The Return of Christ

Pre- or post-tribulation rapture and what it means for the Church

Brian Hills

© 2012 Brian Hills. All rights reserved.

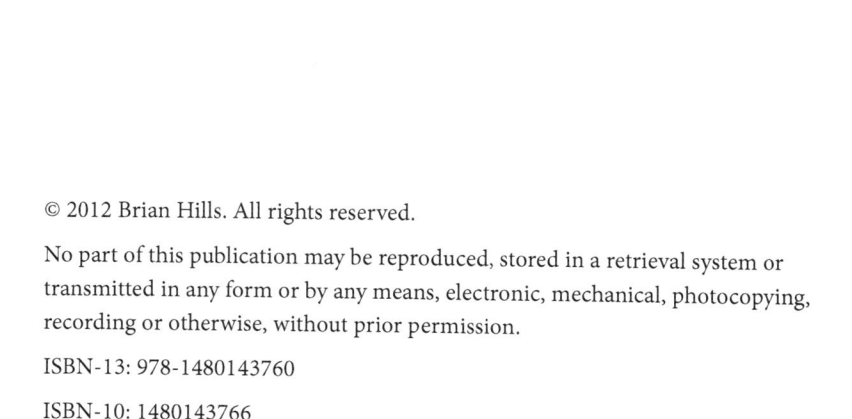

No part of this publication may be reproduced, stored in a retrieval system or transmitted in any form or by any means, electronic, mechanical, photocopying, recording or otherwise, without prior permission.

ISBN-13: 978-1480143760

ISBN-10: 1480143766

This book is dedicated to my loving wife, Kathrin, for her faithful support and to my daughter, Elizabeth, and son-in-law, Alex, for their proofreading and encouragement. Special thanks go to my son, Daniel, for getting the book to print.

This book is dedicated to that future generation of Christians who face the fulfillment of the Biblical prophesies.

Contents

Author's preface	7
Chapter 1. We are in the End Times	11
1.1 The signs of the End Times	12
1.2 Two unfulfilled signs of the End Times	13
1.3 The Signs and the Seals	15
1.4 Rapture of the worldwide Church	20
Chapter 2. The rise of the Antichrist	27
2.1 Daniel's vision of the five earthly empires	28
2.2 Daniel's vision of the four beasts	30
2.3 Daniel's vision of the Ram and the He-goat	33
2.4 Daniel's vision of the seventy weeks of years	35
2.5 The attempted assassination of the Antichrist	37
Chapter 3. Armageddon and the demise of the Antichrist	41
3.1 Gathering the armies for the battle of Armageddon	41
3.2 The demise of the Antichrist and False Prophet	44
3.3 The conversion of the Jewish nation	45
Chapter 4. The Millennium reign of Christ and the final rebellion	49
4.1 Peace and mass evangelism during the Millennium reign of Christ	50
4.2 Thrones in heaven and the first resurrection	52
4.3 The end of the Millennium and Satan's final rebellion	54

Chapter 5. The end events   57
5.1 The destruction of the Cosmos   57
5.2 The Second Resurrection and the Great White Throne Judgment   58
5.3 The New Creation and the New Jerusalem   61
5.4 The City of Babylon and the Harlot of the Antichrist   65

Chapter 6. Symbolism and chronology in the book of Revelation   69
6.1 Repeated timelines   69
6.2 The seven trumpets   71
6.3 The seven mystic figures   80
6.4 The seven bowls of wrath   84
6.5 The two witnesses   90
6.6 Preparing today's Church   92

Chapter 7. Epilogue   95

Author's preface

Forty years ago, as a young man in my twenties, I was researching in theoretical physics at the Massachusetts Institute of Technology (M.I.T.) in Boston, USA with the financial support of a NATO post-doctoral research fellowship. It was at that time that I asked Jesus into my life and became a Christian, which was the best decision I have ever made. Being an academic it was not long before I started thinking about Biblical eschatology, which is a fancy theological name for prophetic studies of the future of mankind and planet Earth. Biblical eschatology in the USA at that time seemed to be dominated by "pre-tribulation rapture" theology which proposed that the worldwide Church will be suddenly caught up into the air to be with Jesus, (i.e. raptured) before the Great Tribulation of the Antichrist begins. The Church therefore escapes persecution, which, of course, is a pleasant and desirable interpretation of scripture. After all, who wants to live through the Antichrist's persecution? It is not, therefore, surprising that, even today, the "Left Behind" series of books and DVD's written by Tim LaHaye and Jerry Jenkins who advocate pre-tribulation rapture remain very popular, having sold over 40 million products since it was first published in 1995. As a young Christian working in the USA those forty years ago, I also eagerly, and somewhat uncritically, embraced this interpretation of end-time events. However over the years, as I have contemplated the word of God, my opinion has changed and I now believe that pre-tribulation rapture, though very comforting, is mistaken. God does not usually remove his people from persecution. Instead we find numerous scriptures warning us that if we live godly lives in Jesus then we should not be surprised if, like Jesus, we are hated and reviled and I personally find no strong scriptural basis for thinking that the Great Tribulation should be an exception. I have therefore written this book to present the case for post-tribulation rapture, where the Church, unfortunately, has to experience the Great Tribulation of the Antichrist before it is raptured. Because this is not a very pleasant scenario I do not expect this book to be a best seller, but seeking the truth has always been my primary motivation, not popularity, nor making money from book sales.

Despite my belief in post-tribulation rapture no one can be dogmatic so I try to keep an open mind to reasoned argument. Likewise, I would also ask readers not to accept my opinion as the truth in an uncritical way, but to read my arguments then search the scriptures for themselves and come to their own conclusions. There is no substitute for first-hand scriptural knowledge when it comes to defending the faith, especially if our walk with Jesus leads to persecution. I cannot help thinking that Christians in the USA and Western Europe, who, like me, have never experienced persecution, are the exception and not the rule. Indeed Christians in many Islamic countries as well as in North Korea and China, Vietnam and Laos are experiencing persecution right now. Hinduism extremism is persecuting Christians in India and Nepal and the history of the Church has been characterised by waves of persecution since the Lord's ascension. Indeed the first three centuries of the Church until the time of Constantine were characterised by extreme persecution under the Roman emperors. Because we, in the Western Church are separated from these events in space and time it is easy for us to think that our situation is the norm and that persecution is the exception, a viewpoint that is reinforced by pre-tribulation rapture theology. However I personally think that this is an illusion and that this period of relative tranquility in the Western church is temporary and will, over the next few years, be drawing to a close, especially in Britain, where I see the increasing prioritisation of other faiths as well as the rising tide of political correctness trying to conform the church to secular humanistic values, in contradiction to God's word.

Another cause for concern is that, for Christians, pre-tribulation rapture theology tends to take away the sense of urgency that the Church needs to get prepared for tough times ahead. If we really believe that the Lord will remove us before the Great Tribulation then the incentive to train as full-equipped soldiers of Christ ready for spiritual warfare is greatly reduced and there is a danger of getting lulled into a false sense of security. I have therefore written this book not so much as theological exercise in eschatology but as a call to the Church to get prepared for the End Times in obedience to the Lord's appeal to us,

"Therefore you also must be ready; for the Son of man is coming at an hour you do not expect." Matthew 24:44

Finally I should say that if readers are looking for detailed predictions of what year the Lord will return or the identity of the Antichrist or to make close correspondences between current political shifts and the book of Revelation, they will be disappointed because this is not my intention in writing this book. Rather my motive is to present the case for post-tribulation rapture and, above all, to encourage the reader to get prepared by studying the scriptures for themselves and not neglecting books like Revelation, even though they may be difficult to interpret.

All scriptural quotations are taken from the Revised Standard Version.

Brian Hills, D.Phil.,

Norwich, UK,
September 2012.

Chapter 1.

We are in the End Times

Although we live in the here and now it is important that we also maintain what could be called an "eternal perspective". One way of doing this is to remind ourselves that Jesus is coming back again to planet Earth and to look out for the "Signs of the End Times" which are the series of events that Jesus said must take place before he returns. These signs are described in the Olivet discourse and in the book of Revelation and were given by Jesus as an exhortation for us to watch and be prepared. Indeed Jesus said,

"Watch therefore, for you do not know on what day your Lord is coming." Matthew 24:42

and again,

"Watch therefore, for you know neither the day nor the hour"
Matthew 25:13

Moreover, the whole book of Revelation is written so that we Christians would know what is soon going to happen. We read,

"The Revelation of Jesus Christ, which God gave him to show to his servants what must soon take place." Revelation 1:1

Clearly Jesus wants us, his servants, to be wise by making the most of the time. When I look up at the sky I often think of that day when heavens glory will light up the whole earth and every eye will see our glorious Lord. I doubt that I myself will live long enough in the flesh to see that day, but perhaps my son and daughter will live to see it, or, if not them, then perhaps the next generation. It is with this thought that I have written this book so they and future generations of Christians will "be prepared and constantly watching for the signs of the End Times" to which we now turn.

1.1 The signs of the End Times

The Olivet discourse, which is found in Matthew chapter 24, tells us that as Jesus was sitting on the Mount of Olives overlooking Jerusalem his disciples came to him asking what signs would indicate his return and the end of the age. We read,

"As he sat on the Mount of Olives, the disciples came to him privately, saying. "Tell us, when will this be, and what will be the sign of your coming and of the close of the age?" Matthew 24:3

After warning them not to heed false Christs, Jesus answers them by describing the signs of the End Times:

"...You will hear of wars and rumors of wars; see that you are not alarmed; for this must take place, but the end is not yet. For nation will rise against nation, and kingdom against kingdom, and there will be famines and earthquakes in various places: all this is but the beginning of the birth-pangs. Then they will deliver you up to tribulation, and put you to death; and you will be hated by all nations for my names sake. And then many will fall away and betray one another, and hate one another. And many false prophets will arise and lead many astray. And because wickedness is multiplied most men's love will grow cold. But he who endures to the end will be

saved. And this gospel of the kingdom will be preached throughout the whole world, as a testimony to all nations; and then the end will come." Matthew 24:6-14

The reference to wickedness being multiplied in the End Times is also found in the apostle Paul's second letter Timothy:

"But understand this that in the last days there will come times of stress. For men will be lovers of self, lovers of money, proud, arrogant, abusive, disobedient to their parents, ungrateful, unholy, inhuman, implacable, slanderers, profligates, fierce, haters of good, treacherous, reckless, swollen with conceit, lovers of pleasure rather than lovers of God, holding the form of religion, but denying the power of it." 2 Timothy 3:1-5

Jesus also refers to "birth pangs", and one wonders whether he was thinking of the birth of a new age of peace on earth, called the Millennium reign of Christ, or of his eternal heavenly kingdom. We will have much more to say about the Millennium age in later chapters. Meanwhile we see that the Olivet signs, in order, are

1) War 2) Famines 3) Earthquakes (natural disasters) 4) Persecution of Christians 5) Increasing wickedness and selfishness, and 6) Evangelisation of all nations throughout the world.

Then there is a final sign, which is the appearance of the person of the Antichrist, because in the very next verse we read,

"So when you see the desolating sacrilege spoken of by the prophet Daniel, standing in the holy place … then there will be great tribulation such as has not been from the beginning of the world until now, no and never shall be" Matthew 24:15 & 21

1.2 Two unfulfilled signs of the End Times

The first five signs, namely war, famine, earthquakes (natural disasters), persecution of Christians and increasing wickedness have been with us since the first advent of Christ so they are indeed *"birth pangs of a new age"* but cannot be used as indicators of the imminent return of Christ. However, in post-tribulation rapture theology there remain two specific signs that have yet to be fulfilled and which the Lord identified as heralding his return. The first refers to worldwide evangelism:

"And this gospel of the kingdom will be preached throughout the whole world, as a testimony to all nations; and then the end will come." Matthew 24:14

Reference to the book "Operation World" (P. Johnstone and J. Mandryk, Paternoster Publishing) shows that this task is indeed close to fulfillment but is not yet complete. The extent of the unfinished task of world evangelism is hard to quantify because it depends to some extent on how one classifies unevangelised people groupings and how large the church in those groups needs to be to fulfill the criterion that there is a significant witness. These things can only be truly judged by the Lord Himself, but according to Operation World there is no country without a Christian witness and only ten without a visible congregation of indigenous believers (8 in Asia and 2 in Africa). There are 18 countries with a resident Christian congregation of less than 1% and a further 22 with less than 5%. This suggests that we are indeed living in the End Times, but that this sign has not yet been completed.

The second sign that has yet to be fulfilled in post-tribulation rapture theology is the manifestation of the Antichrist. We will examine what scripture has to say about this person in the next two chapters but according to the Lord's statement in Matthew 24: 15 this Antichrist will stand in the holy place (the golden-domed Temple Mount in Jerusalem) and this will be the sign that the Great Tribulation for all believers is soon to start and it will set in motion a series of events that leads to the Lord's return, each of which will be discussed in later chapters.

1.3 The Signs and the Seals

The Olivet description of the end signs has strong similarities to the vision of the seven seals that bind the scroll described in the book of Revelation, chapter 5. This scroll would be familiar to Jewish readers because it represents a legal document – a Will containing a written description of an inheritance. In Revelation this inheritance is the birthright of mankind to dwell in heaven with God for all eternity, but the tragedy is that this birthright was forfeited when Adam and Eve sinned in the Garden of Eden. It is no wonder that the apostle John weeps because no one was found worthy to break the seals and open the scroll, thereby allowing mankind back into heaven. But the triumphant message of Revelation chapter 5 is that Jesus, the Lamb of God, is worthy to break the seven seals and open the scroll permitting those of mankind who believe in him to be saved. However, as far as the end-time signs are concerned it is obvious that the scroll cannot be opened without breaking the seals and we discover that these seals describe events on earth that must take place before the end, so it is not surprising that many of the seals also correspond to the signs of the End Times in the Olivet discourse. There is not, of course, a simple one-to-one correspondence because the seals are not necessarily all signs. So let us examine the seven seals as they are listed in Revelation chapter 6:

Seal 1. The rider on a white horse

"And I (John) saw, and behold, a white horse, and its rider had a bow, and a crown was given to him, and he went out conquering and to conquer." Revelation 6:2

This seal clearly symbolises war because we are told that the rider "went out conquering and to conquer". It therefore corresponds to the first sign in the Olivet discourse though it is not specific to the End Times because mankind has been waging war throughout history.

Seal 2. The rider on a red horse

"And out came another horse, bright red; its rider was permitted to take peace from the earth. So that men should slay one another; and he was given a great sword." Revelation 6:4.

This clearly symbolises all forms of violence… murder, torture, terrorism and lawless criminality that takes peace away from civilised society. We know this because we are told, *"its rider was permitted to take peace from the earth, so that men should slay one another; and he was given a great sword"*. This was not mentioned as a separate sign by Jesus in the Olivet discourse probably because it is subsumed under sign 5 *"increasing wickedness"* because this inevitably leads to increasing hatred resulting in violence, anger and revenge that makes men's love grow cold.

Seal 3. The rider on a black horse

"And I saw, and behold, a black horse, and its rider had a balance in his hand; and I heard what seemed to be a voice in the midst of the four living creatures saying, "A quart of wheat for a denarius, and three quarts of barley for a denarius; but do not harm oil and wine". Revelation 6:5-6

This symbolises famine and corresponds to the second sign in the Olivet discourse. The phrase "A quart of wheat for a denarius, and three quarters of barley for a denarius" describes famine conditions because a denarius was a days wage.

Seal 4. The rider on a pale horse

"And I saw, and behold, a pale horse, and its rider was Death, and Hades followed him; and they were given power over a fourth of the earth, to kill with sword, and with famine and with pestilence and by wild beasts of the earth." Revelation 6:7-8

Jesus did not name this seal as a separate sign in the Olivet discourse probably because death is one inevitable consequence of the other signs, namely war, violence, famine and natural disasters.

Seal 5. Christian martyrdom

"When he opened the fifth seal, I saw under the altar the souls of those who had been slain for the word of God and for the witness they had borne." Revelation 6:9

Martyrdom falls within the forth sign of the Olivet discourse, "persecution", and emphasises that living a godly and faithful life in Jesus will often lead to tribulation and martyrdom. God does not always choose to remove us from such persecution, but promises that we will be greatly rewarded,

"Blessed are you when men revile you and persecute you and utter all kinds of evil against you falsely on my account. Rejoice and be glad, for your reward is great in heaven, for so men persecuted the prophets who were before you." Matthew 5:11-12

The apostle Peter also tells us not to be surprised when such persecution arises, because it is really the normal response of a sin-sick world to godly living:

"Beloved, do not be surprised at the fiery ordeal which comes upon you to prove you, as though something strange were happening to you. But rejoice in so far as you share Christ's sufferings, that you may also rejoice and be glad when his glory is revealed."
1 Peter 4:12-13

There is therefore little scriptural justification for thinking that God will remove the whole of his Church from the Antichrist's Great Tribulation in rapture as in the pre-tribulation scenario.

Seal 6. A great earthquake

"When he opened the sixth seal, I (John) looked, and behold, there was a great earthquake; and the sun became black as sackcloth, the full moon became like blood, and the stars of the sky fell to earth as the fig tree sheds its winter fruit when shaken by the gale; the sky vanished like a scroll that is rolled up, and every mountain and island was removed from its place." Revelation 6:12-14

This language is reminiscent of the third sign of the Olivet discourse and describes a great earthquake that affects the whole globe causing terrifying natural disasters. Although many of us are tempted to try to give a logical geophysical interpretation to this description we must not forget that it is apocalyptic language describing the wrathful judgment of God on a sin-sick world. Nevertheless a logical explanation is, perhaps, possible because we know that if the earthquake is sufficiently severe it could cause volcanic eruptions spewing clouds of dust and ash into the upper atmosphere that would darken the sun and moon. The earth tremors on the night side of the earth would cause the inhabitants there to see the stars apparently shaken in their places. The mountains and islands would be shaken by the earthquake and aftershocks. Regardless of any such 'natural' explanation it is also clear that the description is reminiscent of the apocalyptic language of Joel and Isaiah. In Joel we read,

"And I will give portents in the heavens and on the earth, blood and fire and columns of smoke. The sun shall be turned to darkness and the moon to blood, before the great and terrible day of the Lord comes". Joel 2:30-31

and in Isaiah 34:4 we find very similar apocalyptic language,

"All the host of heaven shall rot away, and the skies will roll up like a scroll. All their host shall fall, as leaves fall from the vine, like leaves falling from a fig tree" Isaiah 34:4.

As we shall discuss in chapter 6, a worldwide earthquake will also devastate the Antichrist's kingdom, but it is unclear whether this sixth seal refers to that particular event. It is comforting to know that this sixth seal also includes God's assurance to his servants that although, as inhabitants of earth they will need to experience these seals and signs, nevertheless His wrath is not directed at them but at the unrepentant of humanity who have rejected His freely offered gift of salvation in Jesus Christ. He will seal his servants with the Holy Spirit who is the guarantee of their inheritance to eternal life, though some will suffer martyrdom (the 5th seal) and many will suffer hunger and thirst (Revelation 7:16), tribulation and poverty (Rev: 2:9-11). We read,

"Then I saw another angel ascend from the rising of the sun, with the seal of the living God, and he called with a loud voice to the four angels who had the power to harm earth and sea, saying 'Do not harm the earth or the sea or the trees, till we have sealed the servants of our God upon their foreheads.' And I heard the number of the sealed, a hundred and forty-four thousand sealed, out of the every tribe of the sons of Israel." Revelation 7:2-4

There has been controversy over the identity of these 144,000, some arguing that they refer literally only to the Jews, and not to Christians. But such an interpretation contradicts New Testament teaching that in Christ there is neither Jew nor Gentile. Moreover the apostles often assign the characteristics of the Jewish people in the Old Testament to the Church. For example, Peter refers to the Church as the *"exiles of the Dispersion"* and as a *"Chosen race, a royal priesthood, a holy nation, God's own people"* equivalent to the description of the Jews in Exodus 19:6,

"...and you shall be to me a kingdom of priests and a holy nation"
Exodus 19:6

Undoubtedly therefore, the servants of God in Revelation are all people, both Jews and Gentiles from all tribes of the earth who have received Jesus into their lives as their Lord and Saviour. Some commentators also puzzle over the number, 144,000, some even taking it literally to mean that a person who is number 144,001 will be excluded from heaven! But this is hardly a necessary or reasonable interpretation. Throughout scripture the number 12 symbolises the organisational completeness and perfection of God's plan. God took 12 × 12 hours (6 days) in the Genesis account of creation (not to be taken literally, but to symbolise that His creation is very good and that it is organisationally complete). There are 12 tribes of Israel; 12 apostles and 12 gates and 12 foundations in the New Jerusalem, symbolising the glorified Church in heaven (see Revelation 12: 9-27). So the complete number of the redeemed in Christ would also be expected to be described by the number 12 × 12 = 144; and to emphasise the large multitude of the redeemed the number 144 is multiplied by a thousand corresponding to a *"great multitude which no man could number"* in Revelation 7:9.

Having examined the signs and seals let us now examine how they relate to pre- and post-tribulation rapture theology:

1.4   Rapture of the worldwide Church

One of the key differences between pre- and post-tribulation theology concerns the timing and nature of the rapture. To see this let us examine the descriptions of the rapture in the Olivet Discourse and compare it with other passages of scripture. In his Olivet discourse Jesus declares,

"Immediately after the tribulation of those days the sun will be darkened, and the moon will not give its light and the stars will fall from heaven, and the powers of the heavens will be shaken; then will appear the sign of the Son of man in heaven, and then all the tribes of the earth will mourn, and they will see the Son of man coming on the clouds of heaven with power and great glory; and he will send out his angles with a loud trumpet call, and they will gather his elect from the four winds, from one end of heaven to the other." Matthew 24:29-31

This description clearly makes the following points:

1. This event comes immediately after the Great Tribulation of the Antichrist, not before.
2. It is global in its extent…every eye will see the return of Christ.
3. It will be accompanied by a loud angelic trumpet call.
4. All the elect will be gathered from all over the world.

Note especially that Jesus makes no reference to two separate "return events", one the rapture, the second the defeat of the Antichrist. He refers only to a single return event. Now let us compare this passage with the description of the rapture in 1 Thessalonians 4:13-17, which reads,

"But we would not have you ignorant, brethren, concerning those who have fallen asleep (i.e. died), that you may not grieve as others do who have no hope. For since we believe that Jesus died and rose again, even so, through Jesus, God will bring with him those who have fallen asleep." 1Thessalonians 4:13-14

This passage clearly states that when Jesus returns, he will "bring with him" those (Christians) who have already died. This is reinforced by the following verse:

"For we declare to you by the word of the Lord, that we who are alive, who are left until the coming of the Lord, shall not precede those who have fallen asleep." 1 Thessalonians 4:15

In other words the dead in Christ will rise first and return with the Lord to gather those Christians who are still alive on earth. So we have here a picture where the Lord will return to Earth together with his glorified saints who have already died and been resurrected and glorified, and the angelic armies will also be accompanying Him. The following verses describe this event in greater detail and for the third time we are told that the dead in Christ will rise first:

"For the Lord himself will descend from heaven with a cry of command, with the archangel's call, and with the sound of the trumpet of God. And the dead in Christ will rise first; then we who are alive, who are left, shall be caught up together with them in the clouds to meet with the Lord in the air; and so we shall always be with the Lord." 1Thessalonians 4:16-17

Note the following points identify this event with the same event described by the Lord in the Olivet discourse:

1. It is a global event
2. It will be accompanied by a loud angelic trumpet call
3. All the (living) elect will be gathered from all over the world
4. It clearly refers to the rapture of the Church because it describes Christians being caught up into the clouds to meet the Lord in the air.

Like Jesus, Paul makes no reference to two separate "return events" the first rapture, then a second return to destroy the Antichrist. This last point, that there is only a single return event, is reinforced by Paul's description of the return in the second letter to the Thessalonians, where Paul warns the Thessalonian

Christians not to give up their jobs and gather waiting for the return of the Lord because this "return event" (the rapture) will not happen until after the Antichrist is revealed:

"Let no one deceive you in any way; for that day will not come, unless the rebellion comes first, and the man of lawlessness (i.e. the Antichrist) is revealed, the son of perdition, who opposes and exalts himself against every so-called god or object of worship, so that he takes his seat in the temple of God, proclaiming himself to be God."
2 Thessalonians 2:3-4

This clearly refers to the same event described by Jesus in the Olivet Discourse, where the *"desolating sacrilege spoken of by the prophet Daniel, stands in the holy place"*

Paul then describes how the Antichrist is destroyed by the return of the Lord:

"And then the lawless one will be revealed, and the Lord Jesus will slay him with the breath of his mouth and destroy him by his appearing and coming." 2 Thessalonians 2:8

The Lord's description of rapture in the Olivet discourse and Paul's description in Thessalonians therefore marry together perfectly and describe a single return event, where rapture and the destruction of the Antichrist are one and the same event. Note especially that we have already been told by Jesus in the Olivet discourse that this event will happen

"Immediately after the tribulation of those days (i.e. after the great tribulation of the Antichrist)." Matthew 24:29

These two descriptions therefore give strong support to the post-tribulation rapture scenario and it is very hard to see how a pre-tribulation rapture scenario fits with either of these scriptures without a great deal of unnecessary and elaborate imagination. Indeed, the problems with the pre-tribulation rapture scenario are considerable because it implies, that apart from the fulfillment of world-wide evangelism, which, as we have seen, is a difficult matter for us to judge, there is no clear end-time sign in the pre-tribulation rapture scenario. The end time events are all triggered by the unexpected rapture of the worldwide Church before the Antichrist is revealed. If this is the case then the Great Tribulation applies only to the Jews and to any new Christians converted as a result of witnessing the Rapture of the Church. This also implies the unlikely situation that the Lord returns twice, the first time to rapture the Church and the second time to destroy the Antichrist and his armies. But then this double-return scenario does not fit well with Paul's description of the rapture in Thessalonians nor with the post-tribulation rapture described by the Lord in the Olivet discourse. Moreover the body of scripture shows that persecution is the expected result of following the Lord whole-heartedly, so a pre-tribulation rapture to escape persecution goes against the majority of biblical teaching.

There is one verse in the Olivet discourse that is sometimes used to justify the pre-tribulation rapture scenario, and that reads:

"Then two men will be in the field, one is taken and one is left. Two women will be grinding at the mill; one is taken and one is left."
Matthew 24:40-41

However, one needs to be careful about the context of this verse. The central point of this passage, from verses 36 to 44, is that we do not know the day and hour of the return event, which the Father alone knows. Therefore we all need to be ready and watchful. In practice, making ourselves ready means always abiding in the Lord and making Him the priority in our lives. In the author's opinion, this passage is not, therefore, trying to describe the mechanism of rapture, but rather that one person was not ready and the other was, and the reason the Lord inserted this statement was to encourage us all to be ready. However, I acknowledge that other sincere Christians take a more literal interpretation of this verse. Nevertheless, for the reasons listed above, and others to be discussed in later chapters, it would seem to this author that the case for the post-tribulation rapture scenario is far stronger than that for pre-tribulation rapture. Fortunately scripture has a great deal more to say about these events, and in the next chapter we will examine in greater detail the person and work of the Antichrist.

Chapter 2.
The Rise of the Antichrist

Let us remind ourselves again what the Lord said about the Antichrist in the Olivet discourse,

"So when you see the desolating sacrilege spoken of by the prophet Daniel, standing in the holy place (let the reader understand), then let those who are in Judea flee to the mountains; let him who is on the housetop not go down to take what is in the house; and let him who is in the field not turn back to take his mantle. And alas for those who are with child and for those who give suck in those days! Pray that your flight may not be in winter or on the Sabbath. For then there will be great tribulation, such as has not been from the beginning of the world until now, no, and never will be. And if those days had not been shortened, no human being would be saved; but for the sake of the elect those days will be shortened."
Matthew 24:15-22

It is clear that if we want to know more about this person called *"the desolating sacrilege"* we must delve into the book of Daniel, which will be the main focus of this chapter. But it is already obvious that this desolating sacrilege, the Antichrist, instigates the world's most terrible persecution of the *"elect"* (i.e. God's chosen people, both Jews and Christians). Jesus emphasises the great extent of this persecution by pointing out that if God had not put an end to it then no human being would be saved. Bearing in mind that the present world population is about seven billion and growing, this implies that the Antichrist's Great Tribulation would have extended to the whole world had God not stopped it. One can only imagine that it would have escalated into the use of weapons of mass destruction, perhaps culminating in a global nuclear holocaust or the use of biological weapons that would have swept over all the continents. Fortunately, as we saw in the previous chapter, Jesus puts a stop to this evil madness by his return, which is an event well worth reading again:

"Immediately after the tribulation of those days the sun will be darkened and the moon will not give its light, and the stars will fall from heaven, and the powers of the heavens will be shaken; then will appear the sign of the Son of man in heaven, and then all the tribes of the earth will mourn, and they will see the Son of man coming on the clouds of heaven with power and great glory; and he will send out his angels with a loud trumpet call, and they will gather his elect from the four winds, from one end of heaven to the other." Matthew 24:29-31

This clearly states that His return will involve the whole planet so that everyone on earth will see His return. To a 21st century skeptic, this would appear to be physically impossible since the Earth is a sphere. However we are here describing how the higher dimensional realms of heaven break through into our world so we should not be too eager to dismiss this as a physical impossibility because nothing is impossible with God. Let us now learn as much as we can about the *"desolating sacrilege spoken of by the prophet Daniel."*

2.1 Daniel's vision of the five earthly empires

The prophet Daniel rose to authority in king Nebuchadnezzar's court in Babylon by describing and interpreting the king's first dream, which is described in Daniel chapter 2. The king dreams of a statute with a golden head; silver breast and arms; a belly and thighs of Bronze; two legs of iron and feet of iron mixed with clay. The whole statue was then struck by a stone that was not cut by human hands that grew to become a great mountain that filled the whole earth. As Daniel is told, the statue represents five earthly kingdoms and history assigns these to the following empires:

- The gold head represents Nebuchadnezzar's Babylonian Empire
- The silver breast and arms represents the Medo-Persian Empire
- The belly and thighs of bronze represents the Grecian Empire under Alexander the Great and successors
- The two legs of iron represent the Roman Empire (eventually divided into East and West)
- The feet of iron and clay with 10 toes represents the empire at the end of the age, with the ten toes representing ten world powers (kingdoms).

The stone that breaks the feet represents the return of Christ who destroys the Antichrist and His kingdom (Babylon) and heralds the Millennium reign of Christ that encompasses the whole earth for a thousand years. His eternal kingdom then continues in heaven for all eternity. We may not realise it but this, the first of Daniel's visions, shows that we, in the 21st century, are living in the final empire comprising the two feet of mixed iron and clay. We can only speculate what the iron and clay signify, possibly political and religious power, but, whatever they represent, it is clear that they do not mix so any attempt to form a united world empire in this final era will inevitably fail. The existence of ten toes is significant because in the book of Revelation the Antichrist is described as having ten horns, which are identified as ten kings who receive power as kings for one hour, together with the Antichrist. These kings are of one mind and give their power and authority to the beast (the Antichrist). We read,

"And the ten horns that you saw are ten kings who have not yet received royal power, but they are to receive authority as kings for one hour, together with the beast. These are of one mind and give over their power and authority to the beast; they will make war on the Lamb and the Lamb will conquer them, for He is Lord of Lord and King of Kings and those who follow him are called and chosen and faithful." Revelation17:12-14

It seems reasonable to assume that the ten toes in Daniel's vision are the same as the ten kings in the book of Revelation, but, in the author's opinion it is not yet possible at this point of time to assign the ten kings either to persons or powers or kingdoms, and this is not the intention of this book. Their identity will undoubtedly become obvious nearer the time of their fulfillment. Instead we can learn more about the Antichrist by moving on to the next prophecy concerning him:

2.2 Daniel's vision of the four beasts

In Daniel's next vision four beasts come out of the sea. The first three beasts are easy to assign to world empires such that,

- A Lion with eagle's wings represents the Babylonian Empire
- A Bear represents the Medo-persian Empire
- A Leopard with four wings and four heads represents the Grecian Empire

But then we are told of a fourth beast,

"After this I saw in the night visions, and behold, a fourth beast, terrible and dreadful and exceedingly strong; and it had great iron teeth; it devoured and broke in pieces, and stamped the residue with its feet. It was different from the other beasts that were before it; and it had ten horns. I considered the horns, and behold, there came up among them another horn, a little one, before which three of the first horns were plucked up by the roots; and behold in this little horn were eyes like the eyes of a man, and a mouth speaking great things." Daniel 7:7-8

There can be little doubt that this *"little horn"* is none other than the Antichrist because he has eyes like a man and a mouth speaking great things. Moreover the ten horns are surely the same as the ten toes in Daniel's first vision of the statue and are the same as the ten horns we have just described in Revelation chapter 17. The extra piece of information in this passage is that the Antichrist will destroy three of the horns (kings/earthly powers) in his rise to power. Once again we are told that the ten horns represent ten kings which agrees with the assignment in Revelation 17:12.

"As for the ten horns, out of this kingdom, ten kings shall arise, and another shall arise out of them (the little horn, the Antichrist); he shall be different from the former ones and shall put down three kings. He shall speak words against the Most High, and shall wear out the saints of the Most High, and shall think to change the times and the law; and they shall be given into his hand for a time, two times and half a time." Daniel 7:24-25

Here we learn that the Antichrist will blaspheme, which, as we have seen, agrees with the words of Paul in 2 Thessalonians that, *"he exalts himself against every so-called god or object of worship, so that he takes his seat in the temple of God, proclaiming himself to be God."*

He will also wear out the saints of the Most High, which again surely refers to the Great Tribulation. But here we are told that this Great Tribulation where the saints are *"given into his hand"* will last for *"three and a half times"*. As we shall see, we can deduce the duration of a *"unit of time"* from Daniel's final vision of the seventy weeks of years, where it is identified as a year. The Great Tribulation will therefore last for three and a half years, which is the second half of the seven year rule of the Antichrist and this is confirmed in the book of Revelation where we read,

"And the beast (the Antichrist) was given a mouth uttering haughty and blasphemous words, and it was allowed to exercise authority for 42 months (i.e. 3.5 years); it opened its mouth to utter blasphemies against God, blaspheming his name and his dwelling, that is, those who dwell in heaven. Also it was allowed to make war on the saints and to conquer them." Revelation 13:5-7

This passage suggests that there will be few Christians still alive when Christ returns and rapture occurs...most will have been martyred or will have denied the faith during those terrible three and a half years of the Antichrist's persecution. Those that survive until rapture will be living like refugees and fugitives from the fury of the Antichrist...so their sudden disappearance in rapture will not cause trains or planes to crash (as depicted in some Christian films/novels depicting the pre-tribulation rapture scenario). It is highly unlikely that Christians will be holding professional jobs in the Antichrist's kingdom! We are further told that the Antichrist will think to change the law, which presumably means that he will try to remove the legal restraints to sin in criminal law so that society sinks into a quagmire of unrestrained moral degradation. This is consistent with his devilish character as the desolating sacrilege, the man of sin and the man of lawlessness, because all sin is lawlessness. Daniel also confirms what Jesus declared on the Mount of Olives that the only way that the Antichrist's persecutions can be stopped is by the return of Jesus Himself:

"As I looked, this horn made war with the saints, and prevailed against them, until the Ancient of Days (Jesus) came, and judgment was given for the saints of the Most High, and the time when the saints received the kingdom." Daniel 7:21-22

2.3 Daniel's vision of the Ram and the He-goat

More information about the Antichrist can be gleaned from Daniel's vision of the Ram and He-goat where we learn that he has a bold (fierce) countenance, and, like his father the Devil, understands riddles (mysteries), is cunning and deceitful and that he is ruthless, destroying many without warning. We read,

"...A king of bold countenance, one who understands riddles, shall arise. His power shall be great, and he shall cause fearful destruction, and shall succeed in what he does, and destroy mighty men and the people of the saints. By his cunning he shall make deceit prosper under his hand, and in his own mind he shall magnify himself. Without warning he shall destroy many; and he shall even rise up against the Prince of princes (Jesus); but by no human hand (i.e. God's hand), he shall be broken." Daniel 8:23-25

This description can only refer to the Antichrist because he is broken only by Jesus's return. His knowledge of mysteries, his power, deceit and ruthlessness comes, of course, because he is possessed by all the power of Satan, and this aspect will be discussed again later. A more detailed historical examination of the Ram and He-goat vision also gives an admittedly vague and speculative hint as to the geographical origin of the Antichrist. We are told that the Ram with two horns symbolises the Medo-Persian empire:

"As for the ram which you saw with two horns, these are the kings of Media and Persia." Daniel 8:20

The He-goat symbolises the Greece empire that destroys the Medio-Persian empire, and the great horn is its first king, Alexander the Great:

"And the he-goat is the king of Greece; and the great horn between its eyes is the first king." Daniel 8:20-21

History records that when Alexander the Great died the Greek empire was divided into four parts, under the rule of four kings, according to the assignment,

   a) Ptolemy ruled Greece in the East

   b) Cassandra ruled Egypt in the South

   c) Lysimachus ruled the Seleucid empire comprising mainly modern day Iran, Iraq and Pakistan.

   d) Seleucus ruled Turkey

Hence we read,

"As for the horn that was broken (i.e. Alexander the Great), in place of which four other (horns) arose, four kingdoms shall arise from his nation, but not with his power."

Now it is interesting to note that a certain notorious Antiochus Epiphanes (175-164BC) became a later ruler of the Seleucid empire (Iran, Iraq and Pakistan) labeled c) above. It was he who desecrated the temple in Jerusalem and sought to destroy the Jews. Eighty thousand Jews died in his desecration and he ordered that the Jews should worship Zeus and abandon their worship of God. He entered the temple and erected a statue to Zeus Olympus in place of the altar of burnt offering and stopped the daily Jewish sacrifices for sin. He also entered the Holy of

Holies, thereby defiling it. This identifies him as a type of Antichrist (i.e. not the Antichrist himself, but as a forerunner with the same evil motives). He reigned in Babylon (located in present day Iraq), which suggests, but does not prove, that the final Antichrist will also emerge from the same Middle-Eastern region. This possibility is supported in chapter 17 of the book of Revelation where we discover that the woman called *"Babylon the great"* sits on a scarlet beast with seven heads and ten horns (the Antichrist). However in Revelation *"Babylon the great"* denotes the whole godless world system of politics and commerce as well as all those who worship the Antichrist, and not just the ruined city of Babylon in Iraq. One must therefore be very cautious about trying to determine the Antichrist's geographical origin, but if this author had to make a guess, the Middle East centred on Iraq and Iran would be his first choice.

2.4 Daniel's vision of the seventy weeks of years

This vision, described in Daniel chapter 9 gives a lengthy historical background that need not overly concern us here, but adds the important new piece of information that the seven years of rule by the Antichrist will be divided into two parts of 3.5 years. During the first three and a half years we discover that he makes a covenant of peace with many but, true to his deceitful character, he breaks the covenant after 3.5 years, reveals his true nature and begins his 3.5 years of the Great Tribulation. We read,

"And he (the Antichrist) shall make a strong covenant with many for one week (i.e. one week of years; 7 years); and for half the week (i.e. 3.5 years) he shall cause sacrifice and offering to cease; and upon the wing of abominations shall come one who makes desolate, until the decreed end is poured out on the desolator (i.e. until Christ returns and destroys him)" Daniel 9:27

Further support for the division of the seven years into two parts is found towards the end of the book of Daniel in chapter 12. We know that this refers to the period of the Antichrist because in verse 12:1 we read

"And there shall be a time of trouble, such as never has been since there was a nation till that time; but at that time your people shall be delivered, every one whose name shall be found in the written in the book." Daniel 12:1

This echoes the words of our Lord in the Olivet Discourse. It is then that Daniel asks *"How long shall it be till the end of these wonders?"* (Daniel 12:6) and an angel raises his right hand towards heaven; and replies,

"and I heard him (i.e. the angel) *swear by him who lives for ever that it would be for a time, two times and half a time; and that when the scattering of the power of the holy people comes to an end all these things would be accomplished."* Daniel 12:7

The angel repeats this explanation by declaring,

"And from the time that the continual burnt offering is taken away and the abomination that makes desolate is set up (which many interpret as the beginning of the Great Tribulation of the Antichrist) *there will shall be a thousand two hundred and ninety days* (42 months; 3.5 years)." Daniel 12:11

It therefore appears that this period of two, three-and-a half years is not a symbolic period of time, where the number seven merely signifies completeness, but that it denotes the actual length of time that the Antichrist rules on earth.

2.5 The attempted assassination of the Antichrist

The previous section showed that there seemed to be a step change in the Antichrist's strategy after three and a half years, a change that involves switching from a cunning, deceitful negotiator of covenants of peace with many people, to one where his true nature of ferocious hatred is revealed, resulting in the Great Tribulation. One is therefore lead to wonder what event triggered this sudden change. A possible hint is to be found in the book of Revelation, chapter13, where we read,

"One of its (the Antichrist's) *heads seemed to have a mortal wound, but its mortal wound was healed, and the whole earth followed the beast with wonder."* Revelation 13:3

We are not told when this mortal wound happened, but it may be that it was this that triggered the strategic change. It is also interesting to see how this event mimics the death and resurrection of our Lord and reflects Satan's desire to usurp the throne of God and receive His worship. Indeed Satan seems to be mimicking the Holy Trinity. He himself plays the role of the Father; the Antichrist plays the role of Jesus the Son and in Revelation 13:11-18 we are introduced to the *"Beast from the earth"* who could be called the *"Anti-Holy Spirit"* or the *"False prophet"* who causes the inhabitants of earth to worship the Antichrist mimicking the way the Holy Spirit inspires us to worship Jesus and like the Holy Spirit, it also works great signs. We read,

"Then I saw another beast which rose out of the earth; it had two horns like a lamb and it spoke like a dragon. It exercised all the authority of the first beast (the Antichrist) in its presence, and makes all the earth and its inhabitants worship the first beast, whose mortal wound was healed. It works great signs, even making fire come down from heaven to earth in the sight of men; and by

the signs which it is allowed to work in the presence of the first beast (the Antichrist), it deceives those who dwell on earth, bidding them make an image for the beast which was wounded by the sword and yet lived; and it was allowed to give breath to the image of the beast so that the image of the beast should even speak, and to cause those who would not worship the beast to be slain. Also it causes all, both small and great, both rich and poor, both free and slave, to be marked on the right hand or the forehead, so that no one can buy or sell unless he has the mark, that is the name of the beast or of its name. This calls for wisdom: let him who has understanding reckon the number of the beast, for it is a human number, its number is six hundred and sixty-six." Revelation 13:11-18

Given the existence of this *"Anti-Holy Spirit"* it is not surprising that Satan will also try to mimic the death and resurrection of Jesus through the mortal wounding and healing of his Antichrist. Even the infamous 666 mark ties in nicely with the concept of the Anti-Holy Trinity because, if one were asked to assign a symbolic number to the true Holy Trinity it would undoubtedly be 777 denoting a three-fold completeness; so it is not surprising that a devilish trinity would be assigned a sinful imperfect human number, namely 666. It is sobering that unless a person has this mark on their hand or forehead they can neither buy nor sell, which means, once again, that the persecuted saints in the Great Tribulation cannot partake in the Antichrist's commercial society but, as we have discussed before, they will need to live as refugees, bartering and begging for their survival.

Before ending this chapter it is important to note that none of the prophesies in the book of Daniel ever once mentioned the central point of pre-tribulation theology, namely that the Antichrist, alias the little horn, would arise after the *"Holy Ones, or Saints"* are miraculously and suddenly removed from the earth.

Such a spectacular global event instigating the rise to power of the Antichrist would surely have warranted mention. Instead the rise of the Antichrist in the book of Daniel is described in terms of the political flow of human history as merely one of the horns (kings) that usurps others and flatters his way to power. This, in the author's opinion, lends further support for the post-tribulation rapture scenario. In the next chapter we will see that the post-tribulation scenario with its single return event also explains the final demise of the Antichrist and the False Prophet as well as the mass conversion of the Jewish nation.

Chapter 3.

Armageddon and the demise of the Antichrist

The demise of the Antichrist in post-tribulation rapture theology is associated with three simultaneous occurrences all triggered by the sudden return of the Lord Jesus. The first is the rapture of the worldwide Church, or rather of the few remaining survivors of the Antichrist's Great Tribulation. The second is the destruction of the Antichrist, the False Prophet and their armies in the battle of Armageddon and the third is the mass conversion of the Jewish nation as they finally realise that their long-awaited Messiah is none other than Jesus. It is this third aspect that creates a major distinction between the pre- and post-tribulation rapture scenarios so in this chapter we will also explore what scripture has to say about this conversion event is some detail.

3.1 Gathering the armies for the battle of Armageddon

The Great Tribulation of the Antichrist reaches a climax when he gathers the armies of the world to commit genocide, the complete extermination of all those who refuse to worship him, both Christians and Jews. This is described in Revelation chapter 16:

"And I (John) saw, issuing from the mouth of the dragon (the Devil) *and from the mouth of the beast* (the Antichrist) *and from the mouth of the False Prophet* (the Anti-Holy Spirit), *three foul spirits like frogs; for they are demonic spirits, performing signs, who go abroad to the kings of the whole world, to assemble them for battle on the great day of God the Almighty. ("Lo I am coming like a thief! Blessed is he who is awake, keeping his garments that he may not go naked and be seen exposed!"). And they assembled them at the place which is called in Hebrew Armageddon."*
Revelation 16:13-16

Once again we see the devilish operation of the *"Anti-Holy Trinity"* in this passage, as the devil, his Antichrist and False Prophet work together in gathering the world's armies. It is also noteworthy that the Lord himself interjects in this particular passage to remind us that that He will be returning like a thief. Now this is surely significant because in pre-tribulation rapture theology Jesus would already have returned *"like a thief"* to rapture his worldwide Church seven years before this impending battle of Armageddon. So his statement that he will imminently return in this passage of scripture would hardly seem to be necessary unless, of course, he had not yet returned, as in the post-tribulation rapture scenario.

The Jews are also well aware of the significance of the battle of Armageddon because, according to the prophet Zechariah it is the time that they expect their Jewish Messiah to return in power and glory to rescue them from their enemies. Zechariah describes how the Messiah will descend from heaven onto the Mount of Olives, just outside Jerusalem, and as his feet touch the mountain there will be a great earthquake that will split the mountain in two:

"Behold the day if the Lord is coming, when the spoil taken from

you will be divided in the midst of you. For I will gather all the nations against Jerusalem to battle, and the city will be taken and the houses plundered and the woman ravished; half of the city shall go into exile, but the rest of the people shall not be cut off from the city. Then the Lord will go forth and fight against those nations as when he fights on a day of battle. On that day his feet shall stand on the Mount of Olives which lies before Jerusalem on the east, and the Mount of Olives shall be split in two from east to west by a very wide valley; so that one half of the Mount shall withdraw northward, and the other half southward. And the valley of my mountains shall be stopped up, for the valley of the mountains shall touch the side of it; and you shall flee as as you fled from the earthquake in the days of Uzziah king of Judah. Then the Lord your God will come, and all the holy ones with him. On that day there shall be neither cold nor frost. And there shall be continuous day (it is known to the Lord), not day and not night, for at evening time there shall be light." Zechariah 14:1-7

The last reference to the fact that on the day of the Messiah's return there will be neither day nor night, presumably because the whole earth is lit by the light of heaven, identifies this event with Jesus's return described in the Olivet discourse associated with the angelic trumpet call and the worldwide rapture of the Church. There is no hint in this passage that the Church has already been raptured and that this is the Lord's second return to Earth. Instead we find only the singular reference that *"the Day of the Lord is coming"*. We also get confirmation that the return will be accompanied by *"all the holy ones"*, which refers to the resurrected and glorified Christian dead, in agreement with Paul's statement in Thessalonians that *"through Jesus, God will bring with him those who have fallen asleep"* (1 Thessalonians 4:14) along with the angelic armies of heaven. The same return event is described in the book of Acts when the disciples witness Jesus's ascension from the Mount of Olives. After Jesus had explained to his disciples that the exact time for restoring the kingdom to Israel was in the Father's hand we read

"And when he (Jesus) had said this, as they (the disciples) were looking on, he was lifted up, and a cloud took him out of their sight. And while they were gazing into heaven as he went, behold, two men stood by them in white robes, and said, 'Men of Galilee, why do you stand looking into heaven? This Jesus, who was taken up from you into heaven, will come in the same way as you saw him go into heaven.' Then they returned to Jerusalem from the Mount called Olivet, which is near Jerusalem." Acts 1:9-12

There is therefore no doubt that the Mount of Olives is where Jesus will return, which is why a famous Jewish cemetery is located there in the belief that they will be resurrected on that mountain by their Messiah when he comes to destroy their enemies.

3.2 The demise of the Antichrist and False Prophet

The demise of the Antichrist and his armies is described in detail in both the books of Zechariah and Revelation. In Zechariah we discover that the armies of the Antichrist are destroyed by a ferocious plague and in panic the armies fight each other:

"And this shall be the plague with which the Lord will smite all the peoples that wage war against Jerusalem: their flesh shall rot while they are still on their feet, their eyes shall rot in their sockets, and their tongues shall rot in their mouths. And on that day a great panic from the Lord will fall on them, so that each will lay hold on the hand of his fellow, and the hand of the one will be raised against the hand of the other; even Judah will fight against Jerusalem." Zechariah 14:12-14

In the book of Revelation we also learn that the Antichrist and False Prophet are not killed but are instead thrown alive into the only suitable place for them - Hell *"where they will be tormented day and night for ever and ever"* (Revelation 20:10).

"Then I saw an angel standing in the sun, and with a loud voice he called to all the birds that fly in midheaven, 'Come gather for the great supper of God, to eat the flesh of kings, the flesh of captains, the flesh of mighty men, the flesh of horses and their riders, and the flesh of all men, both free and slave, both small and great'. And I saw the beast and the kings of the earth with their armies gathered to make war against him who sits upon the horse (Jesus) *and against his army. And the beast was captured, and with it the False Prophet who in its presence had worked the signs by which he deceived those who had received the mark of the beast and those who worshipped its image. These two were thrown alive into the lake of fire that burns with sulphur* (hell)*. And the rest were slain with the sword who sits on the horse, the sword that issues from his mouth, and all the birds were gorged with their flesh."*
Revelation 19:17-21

3.3 The conversion of the Jewish nation

Not surprisingly, the appearance of their long-awaited Messiah descending on the Mount of Olives and defeating their enemies causes those surviving Jewish refugees in Jerusalem, Israel and around the world to rejoice in God their saviour. But far more than that, they also realise, to their dismay, that their Messiah is none other than Jesus Christ, whom they rejected and crucified over two thousand years ago. No wonder Jesus, in his Olivet discourse says that *"then all the tribes of the earth will mourn"* (Matthew 24:30) as they realise their terrible mistake. The extent of the regret among the Jews is well described in Zechariah chapter 12 when we read,

"And I will pour out on the house of David and the inhabitants of Jerusalem a spirit of compassion and supplication, so that, when they look on him whom they have pierced, they shall mourn for him, as one mourns for an only child, and weep bitterly over him, as one weeps over a first born." Zechariah 12:10

"On that day there shall be a fountain opened for the house of David and the inhabitants of Jerusalem to cleanse them from sin and uncleanness." Zechariah 13:1

The earlier reference to *"all the tribes of the earth"* shows that it is not only the surviving Jews who realise their terrible mistake, but all those unbelievers all over the world who are left behind from the rapture and finally realise that Jesus really is the creator of the world. The conversion of the surviving Jewish nation is also described by Paul in his letter to the Christians in Rome when he writes,

"I want you to understand this mystery, brethren: a hardening has come upon part of Israel, until the full number of Gentiles come in, and so all Israel will be saved; as it is written,

> *'The Deliverer will come from Zion, and he will banish ungodliness from Jacob',*
>
> *'and this will be my covenant with them when I take away their sins.'*

As regards the gospel they are enemies of God, for your sake; but as regards election they are beloved for the sake of their forefathers. For the gifts and call of God are irrevocable." Romans 11:25-29

As we shall see in the next chapter, Christ's return heralds the thousand year long *"Millennium reign of Christ"* which is a new era in human history characterised by worldwide evangelism and an unprecedented age of peace, prosperity and righteousness. This new era is only to be expected given the stupendous threefold nature of Christ's return, with the rapture of the Church, the destruction of the Antichrist's armies and the mass conversion of the Jewish nation. In the author's opinion this is another reason why the pre-tribulation rapture scenario fails to be convincing. If just the rapture of the few remaining surviving refugees from the planet in this post-tribulation scenario heralds such a mass conversion of the Jews and of tribes of the Earth, just imagine what the effect would be if billions of Christians from all over the world, from every nation, amounting to perhaps a third of the planet's population, suddenly vanished in the pre-tribulation rapture scanario! Not a single person left behind, whether Atheist, Humanist, Muslim, Hindu or Buddhist would be unaffected and they could hardly fail to realise that Christianity must be the truth. How else could they explain the disappearances? All churches would be empty as a testimony to the truth and all Christian friends and family would have vanished off the face of the planet. Surely, like the mass conversion of the Jews this even greater and more spectacular pre-tribulation rapture event would herald a mass conversion not just of the Jews and but of almost all of the remaining world's population, ushering in a global conversion that could not be contained. But this unlikely scenario is not what scripture describes because there is then no role for the Antichrist and the Great Tribulation. It is hard to imagine how the Antichrist could oppose such a mass global conversion to Christianity. At least to the author this is another argument in favour of post-tribulation rapture and makes the pre-tribulation rapture scenario hard to accept. It also leads us to examine the Millennium reign of Christ, which is the subject of the next chapter.

Chapter 4.

The millennium reign of Christ and the final rebellion

The last chapter described the return of Christ encompassing the three-fold events of the rapture of the surviving remnant of the Church, the demise of the Antichrist and False Prophet and the mass conversion of the Jewish nation to Christ. However, nothing so far has been said about the fate of the Devil. This is described in Revelation chapter 20 where we read,

"Then I saw an angel coming down from heaven, holding in his hand the key to the bottomless pit and a great chain. And he seized the dragon, that ancient serpent, who is the Devil and Satan and bound him for a thousand years, and threw him into the pit and shut it and sealed it over him, that he should deceive the nations no more, till the thousand years were ended. After that he must be loosed for a little while." Revelation 20:1-3

Note that only an angel is needed to bind Satan, such is his weakened defeated spiritual state now that his Antichrist and False Prophet have been removed and his plans are in ruins. Now, for the first time in human history, mankind is free from his lies and deceit. No longer are politicians acting like puppets for his evil schemes. No longer will there be the insane lust for power and territory leading to corruption and war. Instead a new era of peace and prosperity ensues on the Earth and because the Church will have already been raptured, this will be spearheaded by the converted Jewish nation with Jerusalem becoming a centre for world evangelism. Of course the world in the Millennium will not be a perfect utopia because people are still sinful, fallen human beings. The absence of war does not mean that crime and political tensions will not exist during the millennium and we shall see that the Lord disciplines those nations and peoples that remain rebellious. Nevertheless, compared with the chaos and destruction of the Antichrist, the world enters a new era of prosperity and peace.

4.1 Peace and mass evangelism during the Millennium reign of Christ

Some of the most beautiful, poetic descriptions of the peace in the Millennium era are to be found in the book of Isaiah, where we read,

"The wolf shall dwell with the lamb, and the leopard shall lie down with the kid, and the calf and the lion and the fatling together, and a little child shall lead them. The cow and the bear shall feed; their young shall lie down together; and the lion shall eat straw like the ox. The suckling child shall play over the hole of the asp, the weaned child shall put his hand on the adder's den. They shall not hurt or destroy in all my holy mountain; for the earth shall be full of the knowledge of the Lord as the waters cover the sea." Isaiah 11:6-9

In that Millennium era, Jerusalem will become the centre of political power as well as a centre of pilgrimage for all the nations and all war will cease throughout the Earth:

"It shall come to pass in the latter days that the mountain of the house of the Lord shall be established as the highest of the mountains and shall be raised above the hills; and all the nations

shall flow to it and many peoples shall come and say:

> *'Come, let us go up to the mountain of the Lord, to the house of the God of Jacob; that he may teach us his ways and that we may walk in his paths.'*

For out of Zion shall go forth the law, the word of the Lord from Jerusalem. He shall judge between the nations, and decide for many peoples; and they shall beat their swords into plowshares, and their spears into pruning hooks; nation shall not lift up sword against nation, neither shall they learn war any more." Isaiah 2:2-4

Obviously the reference to mountains is symbolic language denoting that Israel will become the effective political power during the Millennium and this is confirmed by the words of Zechariah:

"Many peoples and strong nations shall come to seek the Lord in Jerusalem, and to entreat the favour of the Lord. Thus says the Lord of hosts: In those days ten men from the nations of every tongue shall take hold of the robe of a Jew, saying, 'Let us go with you, for we have heard that God is with you.'" Zechariah 8:22-23

Jerusalem will also become a centre for thanksgiving and rejoicing to the Lord of hosts. In the Jewish calendar the feast of Booths (also called the feast of Tabernacles) is a time when all Jews come to Jerusalem for seven days to thank the Lord for the harvest and to thank him for their deliverance from Egypt during the time of the exodus. In the Millennium this act of remembrance and thanksgiving will be extended to every nation and there will be sanctions on any nation that refuse to obey. We read,

"Then every one that survives of all the nations that have come against Jerusalem shall go up year after year to worship the King, the Lord of hosts, and to keep the feast of booths (tabernacles). *And if any of the families of the earth do not go up to Jerusalem*

to worship the King, the Lord of hosts, there will be no rain on them (i.e. no harvest). *And if the family of Egypt do not go up and present themselves, then upon them shall come the plague with which the Lord afflicts the nations that do not go up to keep the feast of booths. This shall be the punishment to Egypt and the punishment to all the nations that do not go up to keep the feast of booths."* Zechariah 14:16-19

The same theme is found in the book of Isaiah:

" The sons of those who oppressed you shall come bending low to you; and all who despised you shall bow down at your feet; they shall call you the City of the Lord, the Zion of the Holy One of Israel." Isaiah 60:14

4.2 Thrones in heaven and the first resurrection

Whether one subscribes to pre- or post-tribulation rapture, the situation in heaven during the Millennium era on Earth is the same. The dead in Christ have been resurrected and glorified and are united with all those raptured persecuted saints who endured the Great Tribulation of the Antichrist. Revelation describes this united glorified heavenly body as the fruit of the *"first resurrection":*

"This is the first resurrection. Blessed and holy is he who shares in the first resurrection! Over such the second death has no power, but they shall be priests of God and of Christ, and they shall reign with him a thousand years." Revelation 20:6

It is this last statement that *"they shall reign with him a thousand years"* that causes some confusion in the interpretation of this passage, since it begs the question as to who will be reigning with Christ for a thousand years? Is it all the glorified body of Christ in heaven or just a select few? While one cannot know for certain, it seems reasonable to this author that although the whole body of Christ in heaven will be united and involved in the heavenly administration of the Millennium era on Earth, the Lord will give special authority and responsibility to those few saints who faithfully experienced the three and a half years persecution of the Antichrist. Thus we read,

"Then I saw thrones and seated on them were those to whom judgment was committed. Also I saw the souls of those who had been beheaded for their testimony to Jesus and for their word of God, and who had not worshipped the beast or its image and had not received the mark on their foreheads or their hands. They came to life and reigned with Christ a thousand years." Revelation 20:4

It also seems reasonable to assume that the administration of the Millennium events on Earth will be undertaken by Jesus and his glorified church from heaven and not, as some commentators have proposed, from the city of Jerusalem on Earth. Nowhere in scripture is it stated that Jesus will rule the Millennium from the earthly city of Jerusalem and such an idea leads to some rather peculiar scenarios. Imagine, for the sake of argument, that Jesus really was located in Jerusalem during the Millennium reign. What would most of the world's population want to do but travel to Jerusalem to see him, causing absolute chaos. It is true that there is a single verse in Zechariah that could, with a stretch of the imagination, be interpreted in this way:

"And the Lord will become king over all the earth; on that day the Lord will be one and his name one" Zechariah 14:9

But becoming king over the whole earth surely does not require the Lord to be physically located in Jerusalem! There is, however a far more serious question to be addressed: If the first resurrection refers to the glorified Church in heaven, then we need to ask what the "second resurrection" refers to? In Revelation 20 verse

5 we are told that,

"The rest of the dead did not come to life until the thousand years were ended." Revelation 20:5

This, surely, refers to the general resurrection of all the rest of mankind who have not believed the gospel of salvation and this will be discussed in the next chapter. It will include all those people who died physically during the Millennium era so, of course, and we are told that this general or "second" resurrection will not happen until after the thousand years Millennium era on Earth is ended and new events unfold.

4.3 The end of the Millennium and Satan's final rebellion

As we have seen, the thousand-year Millennium era comes to an end when the Devil is released from his prison "the bottomless pit" and emerges again to deceive the nations and cause war and strife. His hateful agenda is unchanged, namely to wipe out the Holy people and destroy Jerusalem. We read,

"And when the thousand years are ended, Satan will be loosed from his prison and will come out to deceive the nations which are at the four corners of the earth, that is Gog and Magog, to gather them for battle; their number is like the sand of the sea. They march up over the broad earth and surround the camp of the saints and the beloved city; but fire comes down from heaven and consumed them and the devil who had deceived them was thrown into the lake of fire and sulphur (Hell) *where the beats and False Prophet were and they will be tormented day and night for ever and ever."*
Revelation 20:7-10

The reference to Gog and Magog is particularly interesting because these are also referred to in the same context in the prophesies of Ezekiel (chapters 38 and 39) given over two and a half thousand years ago. Historically, the land of Magog has been identified with the Goths who occupied large regions north of Israel, in Eastern and Southern Europe and who were instrumental in the fall of the Roman empire, though Magog as a distinct empire disappeared in the middle ages. Magog has also been associated with the Sythians who occupied parts of Central Asia and also with the Russians so the exact geographical origin of the *"Magog"* in this passage of Revelation is a matter of speculation except that we are clearly told in Ezekiel that they will come from the *"uttermost parts of the north"* (Ezekiel 38:6; 15; 39:2). Magog's agenda is as described in Revelation and inspired by the newly released Devil, namely the destruction and plundering of Israel who now live in peace at the end of the Millennium. We read,

"Thus says the Lord God: On that day thoughts will come into your mind, and you will devise an evil scheme and say, 'I will go up against the land of unwalled villages; I will fall upon the quiet people who dwell securely, all of them dwelling without walls, and having no bars or gates; to seize spoil and carry off plunder; to assail the waste places which are now inhabited, and the people who were gathered from the nations, who have gotten cattle and goods, who dwell at the centre of the earth.'" Ezekiel 38:10-12

In human terms Magog's victory over the peaceful and undefended people of Israel would seem inevitable, but God is the defender of his people and, in agreement with the description in Revelation we find they are destroyed by his fire of destruction:

"Thus says the Lord God: Behold I am against you, O Gog ... You will fall upon the mountains of Israel, you and all your hordes and the peoples that are with you; I will give you to the birds of prey of every sort and to the wild beasts to be devoured. You shall fall in the open field; for I have spoken, says the Lord God. I will send fire

on Magog and on those who dwell securely in the coastlands; and they shall know that that I am the Lord." Ezekiel 39: 4-6

The enormous size of the Magog armies is described as being so large it is like "the sands of the sea" and we are told that the wood from their weapons is sufficient for seven years of fuel for the Israelites:

"Then those who are in the cities of Israel will go forth and make fires of the weapons and burn them, shields and bucklers, bows and arrows, handspikes and spears, and they will make fires of them for seven years; so that they will not need to take wood out of the field or cut down any out of the forests." Ezekiel 39: 9-10

It also takes Israel seven months to bury the dead bodies:

"For seven months the house of Israel will be burying them, in order to cleanse the land." Ezekiel 39:12

It is interesting to note that the weapons used by the Magog army are not those of modern warfare such as tanks and machine guns, but primitive bows and arrows, consistent with the early statement that, during the Millennium, nations will not learn the art of war until, once again, they are prompted by the Devil in his final act of defiance.

The removal of Satan and the powers of darkness marks the end of the Millennium age and initiates three new events which are the subject of the next chapter.

Chapter 5.

The end events

The final removal of the Devil marks the end of the Millennium age and initiates three major new events: First, the destruction of the whole cosmos, including planet Earth. Second, the resurrection of all who have died outside of Christ and third, the creation of a new eternal heaven and new earth. Each will be considered in turn.

5.1   The destruction of the Cosmos

The first event, the destruction of the Cosmos, is described in the apostle Peter's second epistle:

"But the day of the Lord will come like a thief, and then the heavens will pass away with a loud noise, and the elements will be dissolved with fire, and the earth and the works that are upon it will be burned up." 2 Peter 3:10

Such is the spectacular nature of this event that it is alluded to by the prophet Isaiah in his ministry about seven hundred years BC:

"All the host of heaven shall rot away, and the skies roll up like a scroll. All their host shall fall, as leaves fall from the vine, like leaves falling from a tree." Isaiah 34:4

In the previous chapter describing the final rebellion we saw that although the armies of Magog were miraculously destroyed by fire from heaven and the Devil was thrown into hell, nevertheless it took seven years for Israel to bury the bodies and gather their weapons, so there is obviously some time gap between the Devil's removal and this cosmic destruction. However scripture is silent about this interim period and whether those on earth will witness it. Obviously these matters are far beyond our limited comprehension and are in God's almighty hands.

5.2 The second resurrection and the Great White Throne Judgment

The destruction of the Cosmos initiates the second major event, namely the resurrection of all who have died outside of Christ to the Great White Throne Judgment as described in the book of Revelation:

"Then I saw a great white throne and him who sat upon it; from his presence earth and sky fled away, and no place was found for them. And I saw the dead, both great and small, standing before the throne, and books were opened. Also a book was opened, which is the book of life. And the dead were judged by what was written in the books, by what they had done. And the sea gave up the dead in it, Death and Hades gave up the dead in them, and all were judged by what they had done. Then Death and Hades were thrown into the lake of fire (Hell). *This is the second death, the lake of fire; and if any one's name was not found written in the book of life, he was thrown into the lake of fire."* Revelation 20:11

This resurrection has been referred to in an earlier chapter as the "second resurrection" to distinguish it from the "first resurrection" which, as already discussed, refers only to the resurrection of Christians prior to the Lord's return to Earth. The first point to emphasise about the Great White Throne Judgment is that it does not involve the redeemed Church. We have already seen that the Church has been glorified in the first resurrection and, through rapture, united with those saints who survived the Antichrist's persecutions. At the time of the second resurrection the Church is therefore in its glorified state with Jesus in heaven and will not be judged for life or death in this Great White Throne Judgment, otherwise the gospel and Jesus's death and resurrection is emptied of its saving power. Instead we are told twice in this passage that the Great White Throne Judgment involves a judgment of works: *"all will be judged by what they had done"*. The fact that there is also a book called *"the book of life"* also shows that there is the possibility that a person can be saved from Hell and be united with the glorified Church if their name is written in that book because their deeds as judged by Christ, merit it. This interpretation is consistent with other passages in scripture. For example, Paul emphasises in Romans chapter 2 that this is a judgment based on what people have done during their earthly lives:

"For he (God) will render to every man according to his works: to those who by patience in well-doing seek for glory and honor and immortality, he will give eternal life; but for those who are factious and do not obey the truth, but obey wickedness, there will be wrath and fury. There will be tribulation and distress for every human being that does evil, the Jew first and also the Greek, but glory and honour and peace for every one who does good, the Jew first and also the Greek. For God shows no partiality." Romans 2:6-11

Because it is Christ himself who will be judging we can be certain that the criterion of judgment will be absolutely fair and just. He will not just look at the deeds themselves but also the heart motives underlying the deeds as well as a person's conscience and their thoughts. Paul emphasises this point in the same passage in

Romans chapter 2:

"When Gentiles who do not have the law (i.e. the Jewish statues and commandments in the Old Testament) *do by nature what the law requires, they are a law unto themselves, even though they do not have the law. They show that what the law requires is written on their hearts, while their conscience also bears witness and their conflicting thoughts accuse or perhaps excuse them on that day when, according to my gospel, God judges the secrets of men by Christ Jesus."* Romans 2:14-16

The Lord also refers to this judgment of deeds at the end of the Olivet discourse in Matthew 25:31-46 where it is described as the well-known "sheep-and goats" judgment, where the sheep are saved because,

"when I was hungry you gave me food, I was thirsty and you gave me drink, I was a stranger and you welcomed me, I was naked and you clothed me, I was sick and you visited me, I was in prison and you came to me." Matthew 25:35-40

In contrast, the "goats" are assigned to hell because they did not do these things.

(Author's note: No reader of this book need ever face this terrifying judgment of deeds at the end of the age. God, through Christ, offers the free gift of absolute forgiveness to every person provided only that they believe in Jesus as their Saviour and ask for his forgiveness. This is the power of the gospel of salvation and was why Jesus suffered death on the cross out of his great love for all mankind. If you have never asked for his forgiveness and asked him into your life as your personal Saviour then I urge you to do so. I never get tired of that famous verse in John's gospel: *"For God so loved the world that He gave His only begotten Son, that whoever believes in him should not perish but have everlasting life. For God sent the Son into the world, not to condemn the world, but that the world might be saved through him."* Jn 3:16-17)

Before leaving the subject of judgment it is worth reemphasising that it is absolutely clear that all Christians are saved and will not be subject to this Great White Throne Judgment, otherwise the gospel would be emptied of its power. However, this does not mean that Christians will not be judged by what they have done in their service for Jesus during their time on Earth…but it will be a judgment for rewards and not for punishment. This "reward" judgment is described by the apostle Paul in 1 Corinthians chapter 3:

"According to the grace of God given to me, like a skilled master builder I laid a foundation, and another man is building upon it. For no other foundation can anyone lay than that which is laid, which is Jesus Christ. Now if any one builds on the foundation with gold, silver, precious stones, wood, hay, straw - each man's work will become manifest; the Day will disclose it, because it will be revealed with fire, and the fire will test what each sort of work each has done. If the work which any man has built on the foundation survives, he will receive a reward. If any man's work is burned up, he will suffer loss, though he himself will be saved, but only as through fire." 1 Corinthians 3:10-15

The last sentence assures us that even if, to our shame, we gain no reward for our service of Christ, the power of the gospel remains unchanged and we will be saved. However a minimalistic approach to our service is surely not the right attitude for any Christian. If we love Jesus then we want to please him regardless of any future reward.

5.3 The New Creation and the New Jerusalem

We now reach the climax of the end-time events with the creation of a new, perfect, eternal Universe where all the redeemed are united with God in the never ceasing revelation of his glory. Perhaps this ultimate purpose of God is most clearly stated in Paul's letter to the Ephesians where he writes,

"For he (God) *has made known to us in all wisdom and insight the mystery of his will, according to his purpose which he set forth in Christ as a plan for the fullness of time, to unite all things in him in heaven and things on earth."* Ephesians 1:9-10

Revelation assures us that this new creation has already been accomplished, not of course in our linear cause-and-effect timeline, but in God's eternal timelessness:

"And he who sat upon the throne said, 'Behold, I make all things new'. Also he said, 'Write this, for these words are trustworthy and true'. And he said to me, 'It is done! I am the Alpha and the Omega, the beginning and the end.'" Revelation 21:5-6

Chapter 21 of the book of Revelation not only describes this creation event but also goes on to describe a *"holy city, new Jerusalem, coming out of heaven, prepared as a bride adorned for her husband"* (Revelation 21:2), which symbolically describes the glorified Church as a city – The New Jerusalem and also as a Bride, the wife of the Lamb of God. The glory of the Church is described, symbolically, as a city in Revelation chapter 21, where we read,

"'Come, I will show you the Bride, the wife of the Lamb'. And in the Spirit he carried me away to a great, high mountain, and showed me the holy city Jerusalem coming down out of heaven from God, having the glory of God, its radiance like a most rare jewel, like a jasper, clear as crystal." Revelation 21:19-11

And to emphasise that it is not the city itself that is important but the love, unity and adoration between God and his glorified Church we read,

"There shall no more be anything accursed, but the throne of God and of the Lamb shall be in it, and his servants shall worship him; they shall see his face, and his name shall be on their foreheads. And night shall be no more; they need no light of lamp or sun, for the Lord God will be their light, and they shall reign for ever and ever."
Revelation 22:3-5

It is even more revealing to contemplate the fact that the glorified Church is also described as the Bride of Christ, the wife of the Lamb, because this says far more about her character. The foremost characteristic of any bride and wife is, of course, love for her husband. God is love, and if the bride is to be united with the Lamb then she also must be love. But throughout scripture, love is far more than some romantic sentiment. It is a characteristic in the bride that has to be developed, tried and tested by life's trials. Indeed, one can almost hear Jesus asking his bride, "Will you still faithfully love me even when you face trials, tribulations and persecutions? Or is your love like the morning mist that quickly fades away when the heat of the sun rises?" This surely, is why God permits trials and tribulations in our lives and will not always protect us from them. He is preparing us to be the faithful, loving Bride of Christ, which is again why the author finds the pre-tribulation rapture scenario that removes the Church from such trials contrary to the intention of most of scripture. As the apostle James writes,

"Count it all joy, brethren, when you meet various trials, for you know that the testing of your faith produces steadfastness. And let steadfastness have its full effect, that you may be perfect and complete, lacking nothing." James 1:2-4.

and again,

"Blessed is the man who endures trial, for when he has stood the

test he will receive the crown of life which God has promised to those who love him." James 1:12

The apostle Peter makes the same point:

"In this (salvation) *you rejoice, though now, for a little while you may have to suffer various trials, so that the genuineness of your faith, more precious than gold which though perishable is tested by fire, may redound to praise and glory and honour at the revelation of Jesus Christ. Without having seen him you love him, though you do not now see him you believe in him and rejoice with unutterable and exalted joy."* 1 Peter 1: 6-8

Likewise the apostle Paul says,

"We rejoice in our sufferings, knowing that suffering produces endurance, and endurance produces character, and character produces hope, and hope does not disappoint us, because God's love has been poured into our hearts through the Holy Spirit which has been given to us." Romans 5:3-5

As Christians we naturally want to be on the "mountain top", of joy and praise all the time, but it is usually in the trials of life that we learn about real love and faithfulness, especially when we do not understand why God is permitting them. During trials it is so easy to question God's love for us and even to think he has abandoned us, or is angry with us. We must never forget that we have an adversary, the Devil, and we are in spiritual warfare with him. We must therefore learn to be strong in the Lord, to stand firm and resist the Devil as a true and faithful soldier in Christ's army. By doing so we are truly preparing ourselves to be the Bride of Christ.

5.4 The City of Babylon and the Harlot of the Antichrist

As already discussed, the Devil mimics the Holy Trinity by considering himself as the Father, the Antichrist as his son and the False Prophet as a type of "Anti-Holy Spirit". But this unholy Trinity also extends to what could be called the "Anti-Church", which comprises all the worshippers of the Antichrist. Just as the true Church is symbolically called the "New city of Jerusalem" and the "Bride of Christ", so the Antichrist's unholy church is called "The city of Babylon" and the "Harlot of the Antichrist". Her characteristics contrast starkly with the Bride of Christ and are described in Revelation chapter 21:

"'Come, I (an angel) *will show you the judgment of the great harlot who is seated on many waters, with whom the kings of the earth have committed fornication, and with the wine of whose fornication the dwellers on earth have become drunk.' And he carried me away in the Spirit into the wilderness, and I saw a woman sitting on a scarlet beast which was full of blasphemous names, and it had seven heads and ten horns."* Revelation 17:1-3

The reference to seven heads and ten horns identifies the beast as the Antichrist, and we see that his harlot is sitting on him, so that the Antichrist supports her. We also read that the harlot *"is seated on many waters"* and this is explained in verse 15 of the chapter:

"The waters that you saw, where the harlot is seated, are peoples and multitudes and nations and tongues." Revelation 17:15

Evidently the Antichrist's unholy church comprises all those people in the world who worship him and have received his mark. It encompasses the whole ungodly world economic and political system that is opposed to God's kingdom on Earth, which is another reason the harlot is likened to a great worldwide city. Not surprisingly, this worldwide unholy church has characteristics diametrically opposed to the Bride of Christ. First we learn that the unholy church is the source of all Earth's evil abominations such as drugs, alcohol, prostitution, gambling, abuse, slavery, and countless other forms of human degradation:

"(She) *held in her hand a golden cup full of abominations and impurities of her fornication; and on her forehead was written a name of mystery: 'Babylon the great, mother of harlots and of earth's abominations.'"* Revelation 17: 4-5

Not only that, but this unholy church is instrumental in implementing the Devil's agenda of persecuting the Bride of Christ:

"And I saw the woman, drunk with the blood of the saints and the blood of the martyrs of Jesus." Revelation 17:6

There is, of course, no love in the Anti-holy trinity, only mutual hate, so it is not surprising that the Antichrist hates his unholy church and abuses and exploits her:

"And the ten horns that you saw (the kings and powers that support the Antichrist), *they and the beast* (the Antichrist) *will hate the harlot; they will make her desolate and naked, and devour her flesh and burn her with fire."* Revelation 17:16

As we witness the continuing destruction and exploitation of the world's resources, the burning of rain forests, the endless consumerism, and the relentless growth of pollution one cannot help think that these things are also a real physical manifestation of the same devilish hate for all things beautiful and good in God's creation. Revelation also tells us that just as the true Church is the temple of the Holy Spirit, so the anti-holy church of the Antichrist is the temple of everything demonic:

"It (the city of Babylon) *has become a dwelling place of demons, a haunt of every foul spirit, a haunt of every foul and hateful bird; for all nations have drunk of the wine of her impure passion, and the kings of the earth have committed fornication with her, and the merchants of the earth have grown rich with the wealth of her wantonness."* Revelation 18:2-3

Here we see that the godless world's commercial system, based on money and profit that makes many people rich is also part of this global "City of Babylon". Of course, at the present time we Christians also need to work and earn money to live in this fallen world, but we must never forget that it is God who is our true provider and he has promised that he will never fail us nor forsake us:

"Keep your life free from the love of money, and be content with what you have; for he has said, 'I will never fail you nor forsake you.' Hence we can confidently say, 'The Lord is my helper, I will not be afraid; what can man do to me?'" Hebrews 13:5-6

We should therefore be content with what we have, and not conform to the godless world's endless desire for money and riches. As Jesus told us,

"You cannot serve two masters; for either he will hate the one and love the other, or be devoted to the one and despise the other. You cannot serve God and mammon (wealth, money and power)*."* Matthew 6:24

Just as the Antichrist and his False Prophet are thrown into hell at Christ's return, so, in Revelation chapter 18 we read about the demise of his anti-holy church. We are not told the timing of this event, but it would make sense if this happened at the same time as Christ's return because then the Millennium reign of Christ begins and life in the Millennium will certainly not be based on crude commercial exploitation and the godless pursuit of Mammon. Of course, this suggestion is speculative because all End Time chronology is in the Father's hands and we do not always need to know the exact timing and ordering of all the apocalyptic events. It is with this thought in mind that we will, in the next and final chapter, consider two difficult and controversial subjects, namely the role of symbolism and chronology in the book of Revelation.

Chapter 6.
Symbolism and chronology in the book of Revelation

Up to this point the interpretation of End Time events has been relatively straightforward in the sense that the order of events follows a logical progression and the events themselves are readily understood. For this reason it was possible to focus attention on the pre- versus post-tribulation rapture controversy and draw conclusions. However, in this last chapter we will look at the role of symbolism and chronology in the book of Revelation, which are far more difficult subjects and the author acknowledges that his viewpoint may be mistaken. Nevertheless it is hoped that the discussion will stimulate readers to contemplate this subject and encourage them in their walk with the Lord.

6.1 Repeated timelines

A cursory glance at the structure of the book of Revelation shows that it does not follow the linear cause-and-effect timeline that we are so used to in our scientific age. Instead seven events are viewed starting from some early point in history and we are taken systematically through them until we finally arrive in a victorious vision of heaven. The seven events are grouped together and are all characterised by a particular "theme" such as "spiritual warfare". This pattern is then repeated with a new theme, such as "God's wrath", again ending up with a vision of heaven. In this way Revelation repeatedly emphasises that despite all the tribulations and woes, Christ's victorious outcome is assured and Revelation becomes a book of triumph over the powers of darkness. We first see this time-pattern in the description of the seven seals whose main theme is to reveal the sequence of necessary End Time events leading up to the climax of the glorified Church in heaven. The seals span the whole timeline of human history describing war, violence, famine and natural disasters until, in Revelation chapter 7, verses 9-17 we end up with the final triumphant vision of the glorified church in heaven praising the Lamb:

"After this I looked, and behold, a great multitude which no man could number, from every nation, from all tribes and peoples and tongues, standing before the throne and before the Lamb, clothed in white robes, with palm branches in their hands and crying with a loud voice, 'Salvation belongs to our God who sits on the throne, and to the Lamb!'" Revelation 7:9-10

This passage also illustrates the important role of symbolism in Revelation. Just as we do not expect to meet Jesus in the form of a literal lamb, neither should be expect to be clothed in white robes or to be carrying actual palm branches in our hands. Scripture itself is the best dictionary for discovering the true significance of these symbols. For example, Revelation chapter 19, verse 8 tells us that,

"'It was granted her (the Bride of Christ, the glorified Church in heaven) *to be clothed in fine linen, bright and pure' – for the linen is the righteous deeds of the saints."* Revelation 19: 8

The palm branches also remind us of Jesus's entry into Jerusalem when the crowds cut them down as a wave-offering of praise (Matthew 21:9, Jn. 12:13). References to palm branches can also be found in the Psalms (Psalm 92:12, 118:27) and illustrate how a good Bible concordance is an indispensible tool for understanding symbolism in Revelation.

6.2 The seven trumpets

We have already examined the End Time events in human history through the theme of the Seals in the first chapter, so we now turn to the "trumpet theme". It seems (at least to this author) that in the trumpet theme described in Revelation chapter 8 we return to an earlier time and view all of history again but now with a new theme, which is the "wrath of God" directed against all the evil destroying his creation. The first four trumpets describe God's indignation at how the planet (land, sea, fresh water and the atmosphere) is being damaged by the powers of darkness over the span of human history; while the fifth and sixth trumpets describe the wrath of God against those of mankind who perpetrate evil and yet refuse to repent and receive forgiveness. Although God's righteous wrath is revealed in this trumpet theme we must never forget that his wrath arises because he is a loving heavenly Father who hates to see his creation being destroyed by evil. God's unchanging goodness and perfection is beautifully expressed by the apostle James, who writes,

"Every good endowment and every perfect gift is from above, coming down from the Father of lights with whom there is no variation or shadow due to change." James 1:17

But this same desire for absolute perfection also means that there is a rightful place for anger and wrath directed at all who seek to destroy it, and this is the theme of the seven trumpets:

A. The first trumpet

"The first angel blew his trumpet, and there followed hail and fire, mixed with blood, which fell on the earth; and a third of the earth

was burnt up, and a third of the trees were burnt up, and all green grass was burned up." Revelation 8:7

Evil has consequences and this trumpet describes its effect on the earth. It reminds us of the similar consequence of Adam and Eve's disobedience in Genesis where we read how the earth (ground) was cursed and began to yield thorns and thistles:

"Because you have listened to the voice of your wife, and eaten of the tree of which I commanded you, 'You shall not eat of it', cursed is the ground because of you; in toil you shall eat of it all the days of your life; thorns and thistles it shall bring forth to you; and you shall eat the plants of the field." Genesis 3:17-18

This first trumpet also reminds us of the hail and fire that fell on Egypt that are described in Exodus chapter 9:

"And the Lord rained hail upon the land of Egypt; there was hail, and fire (lightening) *flashing continuously in the midst of the hail, very heavy hail, such as had never been in all the land of Egypt since it became a nation. The hail struck down everything that was in the field throughout the land of Egypt, both man and beast and the hail struck down every plant of the field, and scattered every tree of the field."* Exodus 9:23-25

Fortunately, this passage reminds us that God's wrath is not directed at his redeemed Church but at the powers of darkness. Just as God's message to Pharaoh in Exodus was "Let my people go that they may worship me" this first trumpet is also contains God's warning to the powers of darkness throughout history to "let my chosen people be free to worship me".

B. The second trumpet

"The second angel blew his trumpet, and something like a great mountain burning with fire, was thrown into the sea; and a third of

the sea became blood, a third of the living creatures in the sea died, and a third of the ships were destroyed." Revelation 8: 8-9

The second trumpet focuses not on the land but on the sea. However there is a deeper spiritual significance to this second trumpet that is found in the prophet Jeremiah:

"Behold I am against you, O destroying mountain (Babylon), *says the Lord, which destroys the whole earth; I will stretch out my hand against you, and roll you down from the crags, and make you a burnt mountain."* Jeremiah 51:25

This mountain symbolises an evil destroying power, which the previous verse (Jeremiah 25:24) identifies with the city of Babylon and which we have seen represents the global godless world system of commercial exploitation and power that rapes the Earth's resources and which God will destroy when Christ returns and begins his Millennium. The final destruction of Babylon is symbolically represented as a great millstone cast into the sea in Revelation chapter 18:

"Then a mighty angel took up a stone like a great millstone and threw it into the sea, saying, 'So shall Babylon the great city be thrown down with violence, and shall be found no more.'"
Revelation 18:21

The second trumpet therefore expresses God's anger at Great Babylon, the anti-holy church of the Antichrist. The reference to the sea becoming blood is also found in Exodus:

"Thus says the Lord (to Pharaoh), *'By this you will know that I am the Lord: behold, I will strike the water of the Nile with a rod that is in my hand, and it shall turn to blood, and the fish in the Nile shall die and the Nile will become foul, and the Egyptians will loathe to drink water from the Nile.'"* Exodus 7:17-18

This passage from Exodus shows that, like the first trumpet, the second trumpet contains God's warning to the powers of darkness "Let my chosen people go!" It may be worth noting in passing that some scientifically-minded commentators have suggested that the "blood" could be the result of giant plaques of red-coloured toxic algae resulting from pollution that are known to flourish in the Nile. This alga imparts a red, glutinous texture to the water making it appear very much like blood.

C. The third trumpet

"The third angel blew his trumpet and a great star fell from heaven, blazing like a torch, and it fell on a third of the rivers and on the fountains of water. The name of the star is Wormwood. A third of the waters became wormwood, and many men died of the water, because it was made bitter." Revelation 8:10-11

We now turn from the sea to fresh water. The symbolic reference to a star called *"Wormwood"* shows that there is a deeper spiritual meaning to this third trumpet as well. When, during the time of the prophet Jeremiah, the people of Israel broke their covenant with the Lord and worshipped Baal, the Lord gave them poisoned water (wormwood) to drink:

"And the Lord says, : 'Because they have forsaken my law which I set before them, and have not obeyed my voice, or walked in accord with it, and have stubbornly followed after their own hearts and have gone after the Baals, as their father taught them. Therefore thus says the Lord of hosts, the God of Israel: Behold I will feed this people with wormwood, and give them poisonous water to drink.'" Jeremiah 9:13-15

The third trumpet shows that when mankind defies the Lord's perfect plans and pursues his own planetary agenda there are serious and evil consequences that cannot be avoided.

D. The fourth trumpet

"The fourth angel blew his trumpet, and a third of the sun was struck, and a third of the moon, and a third of the stars, so a third of their light was darkened, a third of the day was kept from shining, and likewise a third of the night." Revelation 8:12

Darkness symbolises at least two distinct concepts in scripture. Darkness usually symbolises evil, where is contrasts with the light of righteousness, but in other contexts darkness symbolises God's anger against evil and it is this aspect that it is being demonstrated in the fourth trumpet. Similar symbolism is found in many of the prophetic writings:

"Behold the day of the Lord comes, cruel, with wrath and fierce anger, to make the earth a desolation and to destroy its sinners from it. For the stars of the heavens and their constellations will not give their light; the sun will be dark at rising and the moon will not shed its light. I will punish the world for its evil and the wicked for their iniquity. I will put an end to the pride of the arrogant, and lay low the haughtiness of the ruthless. I will make men more rare than fine gold, and mankind than the gold of Ophir. Therefore I will make the heavens tremble, and the earth will shake out of its place, at the wrath of the Lord of hosts in the day of his fierce anger." Isaiah 13:9-13

Similar apocalyptic language is found in the book of the prophet Joel:

'Let all the inhabitants of the land tremble, for the day of the Lord is coming, it is near, a day of clouds and thick darkness!" Joel 2:1

The fourth trumpet also repeats God's warning to the powers of darkness "Let my chosen people go!" because darkness also covered the land of Egypt for three days prior in Exodus:

"Then the Lord said to Moses, 'Stretch out your hand toward heaven that there may be darkness over the land of Egypt, a darkness to be felt.' So Moses stretched out his hand towards heaven, and there was thick darkness in all the land of Egypt for three days; they did not see one another, nor did any rise from his place for three days; but the people of Israel had light where they dwelt." Exodus 10:21-23

The fact that there is not total darkness in the fourth trumpet but only a third of the light means that at this point on the historical timeline we have not yet reached the very end – the great Day of the Lord when, at the end of the Millennium he will destroy the Cosmos and judge unsaved mankind. Nor can we ever forget that darkness covered the whole land when God's wrath was directed at the sin that Jesus now represented as he died for us on the cross to save us:

"It was now the sixth hour, and there was darkness over the whole land until the ninth, while the sun's light failed." Luke 23:44

This darkness was not, of course, because of Jesus's sin but because of our own:

'For our sake He (the Father) *made him* (Jesus) *to be sin, who knew no sin, so that in him we might become the righteousness of God."* 2 Corinthians 5:21.

E. The fifth trumpet

"And the fifth angel blew his trumpet, and I saw a star (a demon, later identified as Adaddon, Apollyon, the Destroyer, Revelation 9:11) *fallen from heaven to earth, and he was given the key of the shaft to the bottomless pit* (Hell), *and from the shaft rose smoke like the smoke of a great furnace, and the sun and the air were darkened with the smoke from the shaft. Then from the smoke came locusts on the earth, and they were given power like the*

power of scorpions of the earth; they were told not to harm the grass of the earth or any green growth or any tree, but only those of mankind who have not the seal of God upon their foreheads; they were allowed to torture them for five months, but not to kill them, and their torture was like the torture of a scorpion, when it stings a man. And in those days, men will seek death and will not find it; they will long to die, and death will fly from them." Revelation 9:1-6

The fifth trumpet describes God's wrath on those of mankind who perpetrate evil but refuse to repent and accept God's free gift of forgiveness in Jesus. If these people embrace evil then it is not surprising that evil will enslave and torment them because the Devil and his demons hate mankind and seek only to destroy him. We know from the gospels that demonic possession has been a torment for unsaved mankind for thousands of years, but with this fifth trumpet it reaches a climax. We are reminded that the great city of Babylon (the unholy church of the Antichrist) becomes *"a dwelling place of demons, a haunt for every foul spirit"* (Revelation 18:2) so this fifth trumpet certainly includes the worshippers of the Antichrist, but we cannot assume that it applies exclusively to them. The appearance of the demon locusts is appropriate to spiritual warfare and are like *"horses arrayed for battle with teeth like lion's teeth"* which reminds us of the plague of locusts in the book of Joel:

"For a nation (Babylon, represented by an army of locusts in Joel) *has come up against my land, powerful and without number; its teeth are lion's teeth, and it has fangs of a lioness."* Joel 1: 6

"Their appearance is like the appearance of horses, and like war horses they run." Joel 2:4

In Joel this locust army represents the army of Babylon sent to punish apostate Israel but in Revelation this is a tormenting army of demons attacking unsaved mankind. Perhaps the most notable (symbolic) physical characteristic of the demonic locust is the sting in their tail. So many of the Devil's temptations start off with illicit pleasure but end up in bondage and torment - the sting in the tail. As with the other trumpets, this fifth trumpet also reminds us of the plague of literal locusts in Exodus with God's repeated warning to "Let my chosen people go!":

"Then the Lord said to Moses, 'Stretch out your hand over the land of Egypt for the locusts, that they may come upon the land of Egypt, and eat every plant in the land, all that the hail has left.'"
Exodus 10:12

F. The sixth trumpet

"Then the sixth angel blew his trumpet, and I heard a voice from the four horns of the golden altar before God, saying to the sixth angel who had the trumpet, 'Release the four angels who are bound at the great river Euphrates'. So the four angels were released, who had been held ready for the hour, the day, the month and the year, to kill a third of mankind." Revelation 9:13-15

The fifth trumpet described the demonic torment of men who seek death for release but cannot find it. In the sixth trumpet the demonic forces are permitted to kill a large minority (symbolically a third) of mankind who do not repent of their idolatry, murders, sorceries, immorality and their thefts. As is appropriate to the description of demonic warfare, the description is highly symbolic and it is clear that God, in his mercy, has set well-defined limits on the punishment because we read that the demonic forces are only released at a very specific hour, day, month and year, though we are not told when this is on the historical timeline. The fact that the four angels have been "bound" shows that they are evil demonic powers that are now released to punish unrepentant mankind. We are also told that death comes by three plagues, symbolised as fire, smoke and sulphur but what these really symbolise is not explained - perhaps nuclear, biological and chemical warfare, but we do not know. One might hope that the two-thirds of mankind who witness this sixth trumpet might repent and turn to God for forgiveness and protection but such is the slavery of sin that we read,

"The rest of mankind, who were not killed by these plagues, did not repent of the works of their hands nor give up worshipping demons and idols of gold and silver and bronze and stone and wood which cannot either see or hear or walk; nor did they repent of their murders or sorceries or their immorality or their thefts." Revelation 9:20-21

G. The seventh trumpet

"Then the seventh angel blew his trumpet, and there were loud voices in heaven, saying, 'The kingdom of the world has become the kingdom of our Lord and of his Christ, and he shall reign for ever and ever.'" Revelation 11:15

With the sounding of the seventh trumpet we reach the end of the historical timeline of the trumpet theme and, like the end of the seal theme, we find ourselves with a vision of heaven at the time when the Cosmos has been destroyed, a new heaven and Earth has been created and the time for the Great White Throne Judgment has come:

"The nations raged, but thy wrath came, and the time for the dead to be judged, for rewarding thy servants, the prophets and saints, and those who fear thy name, both small and great, and for destroying the destroyers of the earth." Revelation 11:18

6.3 The seven mystic figures

With the completion of the "trumpet theme" we once again return, in Revelation chapter 12, to an earlier point in human history and start viewing the timeline with a new theme of "spiritual warfare". This is done by highlighting seven "mystic figures" who dominate human history.

A. The first mystic figure – The woman with child.

"And a great portent appeared in heaven, a woman clothed with the sun, with the moon at her feet, and on her head a crown of twelve stars; she was with child and she cried out in pangs of birth, in anguish for delivery." Revelation 12:1-2

Joseph's dream in Genesis chapter 37 identifies this woman as the nation of Israel, which is the "mother" of Jesus the Messiah (the child) with its twelve tribes (stars) who are the descendants of the twelve sons of Joseph's father (Jacob, the Sun):

"Then he (Joseph) *dreamed another dream, and told it to his brothers, and said, 'Behold, I have dreamed another dream; and behold, the sun* (i.e. Jacob), *the moon,* (i.e. Rachel, Joseph's mother) *and eleven stars* (Joseph's brothers) *were bowing to me'. But when he told it to his father and to his brothers, his father rebuked him, and said to him, 'What is this dream that you have dreamed? Shall I and your mother and your brothers indeed come to bow ourselves to the ground before you?'"* Genesis 37:9-10.

The child (the promised Messiah) therefore represents the hope of the Jewish nation and of all humanity so it is not surprising that this child is the main target for spiritual attack by the Devil who is the second mystic figure:

B. The second mystic figure – The dragon

"And another portent appeared in heaven; behold a great red

dragon, with seven heads and ten horns, and seven diadems upon its heads. His tail swept down a third of the stars of heaven, and cast them to the earth. And the dragon stood before the woman who was about to bear a child, that he might devour her child when she brought it forth." Revelation 12:3-4

It is interesting that the dragon, who is obviously the Devil, *"sweeps down a third of the stars of heaven"* which describes, symbolically, how the Devil (ex. Lucifer, Son of Dawn, see Isaiah, 14:12-15) persuaded a large number of holy angels (stars) to join him in rebellion against God, resulting in their instant conversion to demons and the outbreak of spiritual war in heaven (see below). As the gospels record, the Devil unsuccessfully used Herod to try to kill (*"devour"*) the child (Jesus). Despite the child's apparent helplessness, no power in the Universe could have ever destroyed him because he is the incarnate word of God, the Almighty God, the Lord of all. When we Christians face similar spiritual attacks we need to stand on the authority of Christ and resist the Devil and his demons because, as the apostle John reminds us,

"Little children, you are of God, and have overcome them; for He (Jesus) *who is in you is greater than he* (the Devil) *who is in the world."* 1 John 4:4

C. The third mystic figure – Jesus the Messiah

"She (the woman, the nation of Israel) *brought forth a male child* (Jesus)*, one who is to rule all the nations with a rod of iron* (i.e. with justice, not tyranny)*, but her child was caught up to God* (i.e. Jesus's ascension) *and to his throne and the woman fled into the wilderness, where she has a place prepared by God, in which to be nourished for one thousand two hundred and sixty days* (three and a half years)*."* Revelation 12:5-6

We read here how the *"woman fled into the wilderness"* which symbolises the fact that the Jewish nation has suffered persecution throughout history, and every type of Antichrist, such as Hitler, has tried to exterminate the Jews, as evidenced by the holocaust. The existence of Israel as a distinct geographical territory in the Middle East is therefore a modern day miracle of spiritual warfare because it testifies to the fact that "God has a place prepared for her". The ancient Babylonian, Medo-Persian, Greek and Roman empires are now just dusty ruins, but, the small nation of Israel still stands secure after thousands of years, even though it is surrounded by nations such as Iran, that, according to it's president Ahmadinejad, would like to wipe Israel off the face of the planet. The three and a half years time period mentioned in this passage reminds us that Israel will even survive the Great Tribulation of the Antichrist and emerge victorious to evangelise the world in the Millennium period.

D. The fourth mystic figure – the angel Michael

"Now war arose in heaven, Michael and his angels fighting against the dragon; and the dragon and his angels fought, but they were defeated and there was no longer any place for them in heaven."
Revelation 12:7-8

The rebellion of Lucifer together with a third of the holy angels triggered spiritual warfare in the heavenly places between the fourth mystic figure – the angel Michael with his holy angels, and the Devil (ex. Lucifer) and his demons. Little is known about Michael though he is mentioned in the book of Daniel (Daniel 10: 13) as coming to Daniel's aid by battling the (demonic) prince of the kingdom of Persia and in Judaism Michael is regarded as the guardian angel of Israel. It is interesting to note that although God could have put an end to the Devil's rebellion in an instant, He chose to use his angelic warriors to fight in spiritual warfare. In the same way God expects us, his servants, to fight in spiritual warfare with the purpose of training us for our eternal role as the tried-and-tested Bride of Christ. We need to remember that, spiritually speaking, we are soldiers in Christ's army, and he is our commander-in-chief so we need to always be prepared by putting on the whole armour of God, as Paul writes:

"Finally, be strong in the Lord and in the strength of his might. Put on the whole armour of God, that you may be able to stand against the wiles of the devil. For we are not contending against flesh and blood, but against principalities, against the powers, against the world rulers of this present darkness, against the spiritual hosts of wickedness in the heavenly places. Therefore take the whole armour of God, that you may be able to stand in the evil day, and having done all, to stand." Ephesians 6:10-13

E & F. The fifth and sixth mystic figures – the Antichrist and his False Prophet

As we have already discussed in some detail, these two mystic figures comprise the second and third person of the Devil's Anti-holy Trinity. They spearhead the Great Tribulation against the saints, but are cast into hell when Jesus returns.

G. The Lamb on Mount Zion

Like the other themes, the "mystic figure" section of Revelation ends up with a victorious vision of the glorified Church in heaven. The trauma of spiritual warfare is over and we read a description of the awesome praise created by the redeemed Bride of Christ, singing in unity with one heavenly voice:

"Then I (John) *looked, and lo, on Mount Zion* (symbolising heaven) *stood the Lamb, and with him a hundred and forty-four thousand who had his name and his Father's name written on their foreheads* (i.e. 12 × 12 × 1000, symbolising the complete, glorified, redeemed Bride of Christ). *And I heard a voice from*

heaven like the sound of many waters and like the sound of loud thunder; the voice that I heard was like the sound of harpers playing their harps, and they sing a new song before the throne and before the four living creatures and before the elders. No one could learn that song except the hundred and forty four thousand who had been redeemed from the earth." Revelation 14:1-3

As discussed, the 144,000 represent the whole united body of the glorified Church and in this vision they all sing one glorious song of adoration to the Lamb. We are not told the contents of the song but it surely is one of eternal gratitude for what Christ has done for us on the cross, in blotting out all our sins and transforming us into his own nature (symbolised by his name written on their foreheads). No angel, archangel or Seraphim in heaven could sing that song because they have never been redeemed from the curse of sin by Christ's death and resurrection.

6.4 The seven bowls of wrath

The timeline of the previous themes – the Seals, the Trumpets, the Mystic figures all began at an early point in history and worked forward towards a vision of heaven, but the theme of the seven bowls starts during the last three-and-a-half years of the Antichrist's kingdom on Earth during the Great Tribulation. We know this because the theme of the "seven bowls" is to pour out the last of God's wrath in the form of plagues on the Antichrist's kingdom and on the men who worship him and have his mark. For this reason the "bowls of wrath" theme could also be called the "theme of the devastation of the Antichrist's kingdom prior to Christ's return", though this is a rather cumbersome title. Nevertheless it is an accurate description because we will see that prior to Christ's return the Antichrist's kingdom ends up as collapsed and ruined cities throughout the world with an utterly broken commercial system and oceans turned to anoxic blood-like algal plaques, with the Antichrist's followers covered in sores and tormented by heat and darkness. To achieve this degree of devastation the "seven bowl" plagues are necessarily far more intense versions of the seven trumpets and of the plagues used by God against Pharaoh in Exodus.

A. The first bowl of wrath: Sores on men

"So the first angel went and poured his bowl on the earth, and foul and evil sores came upon the men who pour the mark of the beast and worshipped its image." Revelation 16:2

The first bowl of wrath causes the followers of the Antichrist to suffer some of the pain that they have been inflicting on the persecuted church during the Great Tribulation and we are reminded that a similar plague caused boils to break out on man and beast in Egypt during the Exodus (Exodus, 9:8-12).

B. The second bowl of wrath: the sea becomes like blood

"The second angel poured out his bowl into the sea, and it became like the blood of a dead man, and every living thing died that was in the sea." Revelation 16:3

This is the more intense version of the second trumpet and also resembles the turning of the Nile to blood in Exodus. Because the followers of the Antichrist have spilt the blood of the saints, so they are faced with blood themselves. But this time it is not just a third of the sea that becomes *"like blood"* but the whole sea, with every sea creature dying. The use of the phrase *"like the blood of a dead man"* shows that the sea did not actually become real human blood, which would be hard to accept scientifically. It does however support the earlier suggestion that giant poisonous red algae plaques will cover the oceans, making them anoxic to all sea life, and imparting a congealed, red, blood-like texture to the water. One might imagine that the death of all sea life would spell the end of the whole ecosystem and life on Earth, but this cannot be the case because we know that the Earth has to survive another thousand years during the Millennium reign.

C. The third bowl: fresh water becomes blood

"The third angel poured out his bowl into the rivers and fountains of water, and they became blood. And I heard the angel of water say, 'Just are thou in these thy judgments, thou who wast and art, O Holy One. For men have shed the blood of the saints and prophets, and thou has given them blood to drink. It is their due!' And I heard the altar cry, 'Yea Lord God Almighty, true and just are they judgments.'" Revelation 16:4-7

This is the more intense version of the third trumpet and also resembles the turning of the Nile to blood in Exodus. However the statement *"true and just and thy judgments"* shows that the new emphasis here is to show that despite the woe judgments, God remains just and true. God is our loving heavenly Father who is perfect in all his ways and even his wrath is measured, purposeful and never vindictive. Moreover his judgments are always designed to try to bring people to repent:

"God, our Saviour, desires all men to be saved and to come to a knowledge of the truth." 1 Timothy 2:4

The following passage is therefore probably the most severe warning in the whole of scripture and is directed specifically at the Antichrist's "anti-holy church" in a final attempt to save them from a fate that is worse than death:

"If anyone worships the beast and its image, and receives a mark on his forehead or on his hand, he also shall drink the wine of God's wrath, poured unmixed into the cup of his anger, and he shall be tormented with fire and sulphur in the presence of the holy angels and in the presence of the Lamb. And the smoke of their torment

goes up for ever and ever; and they have no rest, day or night, these worshipers of the beast and its image, and whoever receives the mark of its name." Revelation 14:9-11

D. The fourth bowl: the fierce heat of the sun

"The fourth angel poured his bowl on the sun, and it was allowed to scorch men with fire; men were scorched by the fierce heat, and they cursed the name of God who had power over these plagues, and they did not repent and give him glory." Revelation 16:8-9

We have already seen how the Antichrist set himself in opposition to every so-called god or object of worship, and even blasphemed by taking his seat in the Temple of God in Jerusalem, declaring himself to be God. (2 Thessalonians 2:3-4). Nevertheless this fourth bowl shows who really is in control of the Cosmos. None of us can fail to be awe-inspired when we see the magnificent images from the Hubble space telescope showing stars and galaxies stretching like dust through the vastness of space, reflecting the glory of the one true God. The blasphemous arrogance of the Antichrist who cannot even create a star is therefore staggering, and this fourth bowl of wrath is surely designed to put him in his place. God alone controls the sun, the solar system and the whole of creation and now he "turns up the heat". Yet the pride and stubbornness of mankind under the grip of the Antichrist makes them curse God for the heat, rather than see the true impotence of the Antichrist, repent and submit themselves to God.

E. The fifth bowl: darkness

"The fifth angel poured his bowl on the throne of the beast, and its kingdom was in darkness; men gnawed their tongues in anguish and cursed the God of heaven for their pain and sores and did not repent of their deeds." Revelation 16:10-11

The fourth trumpet expressed God's wrath by removing just a third of third of the sun's light, but now God throws the Antichrist's kingdom into pitch darkness. Their minds are darkened by evil, so it is surely fitting that they also walk in darkness.

F. The sixth bowl: Demons prepare for Armageddon

We have already discussed this gathering of the world's armies by the anti-holy trinity in chapter 3 so need not dwell on it again. It is amazing that with all the devastation of the Antichrist's kingdom, his priority remains the destruction of the true Church, but that always has been the agenda of his master, the Devil.

G. The seventh bowl: The worldwide earthquake

If the bowls of wrath followed the pattern of the previous themes one would expect that God's wrath would have ended with the sixth bowl and that we would now be lead to a new vision of heaven. However God is not yet finished with the Antichrist's kingdom and in this seventh bowl we find that the cities of the world are destroyed with the greatest earthquake that mankind has ever experienced, resulting in worldwide devastation. The tectonic upheaval resulting in this earthquake is hard to conceive but we are told that it resulted in islands and mountains throughout the world being removed, suggesting that the Earth's topology in the thousand year Millennium will be very different to what it is today:

"The seventh angel poured his bowl into the air, and a loud voice came out of the temple, from the throne, saying, 'It is done!'. And there were flashes of lightening, voices peals of thunder, and a great earthquake such as had never been since the men were on earth, so great was that earthquake. The great city was split in three parts, and the cities of the nations fell, and God remembered great Babylon, to make her drain the cup of the fury of his wrath. Every island fled away, no mountains were to be found; and great hail-

stones, heavy as a hundredweight, dropped on men from heaven, till men cursed God for the plague of the hail, so fearful was that plague." Revelation 16: 17-21

As discussed, "Great Babylon" is symbolic not just of the Antichrist's unholy church (Cf. the new city of Jerusalem) but it also represents the whole godless world system of commerce. The destruction of the world's cities would utterly devastate this commercial system so it is not surprising to read the lament of the rich merchants:

"The merchants of these wares, who gained wealth from her (Babylon) *will stand far off, in fear of her torment, weeping and mourning aloud, 'Alas, alas for the great city that was clothed in fine linen, in purple and scarlet, bedecked in gold, with jewels, and with pearls! In one hour all this wealth has been laid to waste.'"* Revelation 18: 16-17

H. The marriage supper of the Lamb

It is at this point, after the devastation of the Antichrist's kingdom, that we are once again treated to another vision of heaven – the marriage supper of the Lamb with his Bride. In heaven, time is eternal, so we are not told "when" this event occurs, but on our linear timeline it must be after the whole church is united as one body, the Bride of Christ, both through the first resurrection and rapture. Otherwise most the Church would be glorified in heaven but a remnant would still be suffering the persecutions of the Antichrist on earth, which would not make a marriage feast in heaven appropriate. We read,

"'Halleluiah! For the Lord our God the Almighty reigns. Let us rejoice and exalt and give him the glory, for the marriage of the Lamb has come, and his Bride has made herself ready; it was granted her to be clothed with fine linen, bright and pure' –for the

linen is the righteous deeds of the saints. And the angel said to me, "Write this: Blessed are those who are invited to the marriage supper of the Lamb." Revelation 19:6-9

The good news of the gospel is that no one reading this book need be excluded from this marriage feast, you have been invited! You need only believe in Jesus Christ, ask his forgiveness for your sins and ask Him into your life as your personal Lord and Saviour.

6.5 The two witnesses

Although we have considered the themes of the seven seals, the seven trumpets, the seven mystic figures and the seven bowls of wrath, there remains one difficult passage in the book of Revelation that needs to be discussed. It is found in Revelation chapter 11, between the sixth and seventh trumpet, and describes the witness of two servants of God, identifiable as Elijah and Moses, who testify for three-and-a-half years in Jerusalem before being killed by the Antichrist. This places the event sometime in the seven-year rule of the Antichrist, most probably in the later half because he had Satan's power to kill them so by that time his true nature would have been revealed.

In the third bowl of wrath, we have already seen how God gives a severe warning to all to the followers of the Antichrist that if they worship him and receive his mark then they will suffer the eternal consequences of hell (Revelation 14:9-11). Anyone can read this warning in the book of Revelation, but it is highly unlikely that the Antichrist's followers would read it. It is for this reason that God sends the same warning message in the tangible form of his two servants, right in the middle of Jerusalem for a lengthy period of three-and-a-half years. Over that time the whole world would hear the warning and ignorance would no longer be an excuse. Of course, the warning would be hated by most of the

Antichrist's anti-holy church who would do all in their power to kill them. For this reason God gives his two witnesses miraculous power to protect themselves:

"If anyone would harm them, fire pours from their mouth and consumes their foes; if any one would harm them, thus is he doomed to be killed." Revelation 11:5

Given the rich symbolism of Revelation, one would not expect literal fire from their mouths, but a word from God would be sufficient to seal the fate of any person seeking to harm the witnesses. Moreover, God equips them, not just with a warning message and protection, but reinforces the message with divine power to perform miracles. These miracles identify the witnesses as Elijah, who for three-and-a half-years shut the heavens so it did not rain (1 Kings 17:1), and Moses, with the Egyptian plagues:

"They (the two witnesses) *have power to shut the sky, that no rain may fall during the days of their prophesying, and they have power over the waters to turn them into blood, and to smite the earth with every plague, as often as they desire."* Revelation11:6

It is interesting to recall that these two witnesses also appeared conversing with Christ at the transfiguration (Mk. 9:4). The impact of their prophesying was clearly worldwide because after the Antichrist killed them we read that the nations of the whole world refused to bury them so they could rejoice over the corpses which were left for all to see in the street:

"For three days and a half men from peoples and tribes and tongues and nations gaze at their dead bodies and refuse to let them be placed in a tomb, and those who dwell on the earth will rejoice over them and make merry and exchange presents, because these two prophets had been a torment to those who dwell on the earth." Revelation 11:9-10

But, of course, the Lord resurrected his faithful servants after the three and a half days and they ascended into heaven in the sight of all.

6.6 Preparing today's Church

The passage about the two witnesses shows how the Lord has done all he can to warn the peoples of the world not to worship the Antichrist. But I believe that this passage also contains an important message for today's Church. We have seen how wickedness and demonic powers will grow during the End Times so I am convinced that the Church also needs to get prepared by learning to combat the growing darkness by making far more use of the spiritual weapons, gifts and powers that God has already made available to it. In his letter to the Ephesians, Paul prays that the Father may give the Church a spirit of wisdom and revelation in the knowledge of him:

"...and that we may know what is the immeasurable greatness of the power in us who believe..." Ephesians 1:19

Just as demonic powers will increase in the End Times, so it is essential that the Church learns to use the infinitely greater powers that the Father has already made available to us to wage high-impact spiritual warfare. Paul, in his first letter to the Corinthians speaks of the specific gifts that God has given his Church, including working of miracles and healing as well as specific gifts of knowledge and discernment. All too often, especially in today's Western church, a gospel message is delivered but it is not accompanied by the healings, miracles and words of knowledge that would demonstrate the reality of God's power to unbelievers. But these gifts are already available for us. We do not need to pray for them to be given, we just need to learn to step out in faith with the love and authority of Christ and use them, which is all part of our training as good soldiers of Christ. The Lord tells us in the Olivet Discourse that:

"You also must be ready; for the Son is coming at an hour you do not expect." Matthew 24:44

Part of getting ready is learning to use these God-given supernatural gifts already available to us. Another part of the "getting ready" is to prepare the future generation of Christians who will face the Great Tribulation so that, even though they may have to live as persecuted refugees and outcasts, they nevertheless live as fully trained soldiers of Christ, demonstrating the power of the gospel wherever they flee through healings and wonders so that many will come to a saving knowledge of Christ through their witness.

Chapter 7.
Epilogue

We have now completed our brief survey of Biblical end-time prophesies, with no claim for completeness. It has been argued that the case for post-tribulation rapture is far stronger than that for the pre-tribulation rapture and if this is true then there are just two signs that have yet to be fulfilled before the cataclysmic events described in this book begin. However, in this epilogue it is worth mentioning another, more controversial, reason for thinking that the Day of the Lord is near. It is found in Peter's second letter where he tells us that unbelieving skeptics will come in the last days arguing that everything in creation is continuing in its normal predictable "scientific" way, so there is no need to think that Jesus will be returning soon. They argue that two thousand years have passed since the book of Revelation was written with Christ's promise that "I am coming soon", yet nothing has happened and atheistic evolutionary philosophy pervading modern science only serves to reinforce this apathetic viewpoint. So Peter warns the Christians about these skeptics, writing,

"First of all you must understand this, that scoffers will come in the last days, scoffing, following their own passions and saying,

'Where is the promise of his coming? For ever since the fathers fell asleep, all things have continued as they were from the beginning of creation.'" 2 Peter 3:3-4.

Peter then goes on to answer the skeptics by writing,

"But do not ignore this one fact, beloved, that with the Lord one day is as a thousand years, and a thousand years as one day. The Lord is not slow about his promise as some count slowness, but is forbearing toward you, not wishing that any should perish, but that all should reach repentance." 2 Peter 3:8-9

The statement that *"a thousand years* (is) *as one day"* is particularly interesting in the context of Biblical chronology because it suggests (but does not prove) that the End Times really are imminently upon us. To see this we note that, if we add up the number of years as recorded in scripture from Adam to the Abraham we get very approximately two thousand years. It needs to be emphasised that we are using Biblical chronology here where we simply and naively add up the ages of the Patriarchs from Adam to Abraham as stated in Genesis, ignoring all controversies about time gaps in genealogies and calendar changes. We are not therefore referring to the actual passage of time as recorded by a clock. If we do the same from Abraham to Christ we find another, approximately, two thousand years. Then from Christ to the present we have another two thousand years taking us to the beginning of this 21st century. But if, for the Lord, a thousand years is like a day then this amounts to the equivalent of six days of Biblical chronology from Adam to the present. But in Genesis the Lord took a symbolic time of six days to create the world and this was followed by the seventh day of rest - so if the Lord uses the same Biblical time pattern and counts his thousand years Millennium reign as a seventh day of rest, then we reach the conclusion that the Millennium should begin sometime in this 21st century. This is, of course, a very speculative line of reasoning that is easily shot down by skeptics, but it is another reason why this author expects the events described in this book to happen sooner rather than later – indeed within this 21st century. Moreover, when we see the current turmoil in the world with its dramatically rising world population and the diminishing world resources one wonders just how much longer this situation can continue. This present world scenario is surely unsustainable and cannot continue for many more centuries without the events in Revelation changing the situation dramatically. It therefore seems appropriate to end this book by asking the Lord Jesus to come as soon as possible to take control of this runaway world by bringing it into his new age of Millennium peace and righteousness - and perhaps the best way of doing this is to use the words from the last chapter in Revelation:

"The Spirit and the Bride say, 'Come'. And let him who hears say "Come". And let him who is thirsty come, let him who desires take the water of life without price." Revelation 22:17

"He who testifies to these things says, 'Surely I am coming soon' Amen. Come Lord Jesus!" Revelation 22:20

Printed in Great Britain
by Amazon.co.uk, Ltd.,
Marston Gate.